Kaplan Publishing are constantly finding new ways to support students looking for exam success and our online resources really do add an extra dimension to your studies.

This book comes with free MyKaplan online resources so that you can study anytime, anywhere. **This free online resource is not sold separately and is included in the price of the book.**

Having purchased this book, you have access to the following online study materials:

CONTENT	AAT	
	Text	Kit
Electronic version of the book	✓	✓
Knowledge Check tests with instant answers	✓	
Mock assessments online	✓	✓
Material updates	✓	✓

How to access your online resources

Kaplan Financial students will already have a MyKaplan account and these extra resources will be available to you online. You do not need to register again, as this process was completed when you enrolled. If you are having problems accessing online materials, please ask your course administrator.

If you are not studying with Kaplan and did not purchase your book via a Kaplan website, to unlock your extra online resources please go to www.mykaplan.co.uk/add-online-resources (even if you have set up an account and registered books previously). You will then need to enter the ISBN number (on the title page and back cover) and the unique pass key number contained in the scratch panel below to gain access. You will also be required to enter additional information during this process to set up or confirm your account details.

If you purchased through the Kaplan Publishing website you will automatically receive an e-mail invitation to MyKaplan. Please register your details using this email to gain access to your content. If you do not receive the e-mail or book content, please contact Kaplan Publishing.

Your Code and Information

This code can only be used once for the registration of one book online. This registration and your online content will expire when the final sittings for the examinations covered by this book have taken place. Please allow one hour from the time you submit your book details for us to process your request.

Please scratch the film to access your unique code.

Please be aware that this code is case-sensitive and you will need to include the dashes within the passcode, but not when entering the ISBN.

AAT

Q2022

Introduction to Bookkeeping

EXAM KIT

This Exam Kit supports study for the following AAT qualifications:

AAT Level 2 Certificate in Accounting

AAT Level 2 Certificate in Bookkeeping

AAT Certificate in Accounting at SCQF Level 6

KAPLAN PUBLISHING

British Library Cataloguing-in-Publication Data

A catalogue record for this book is available from the British Library.

Published by:

Kaplan Publishing UK

Unit 2 The Business Centre

Molly Millar's Lane

Wokingham

Berkshire

RG41 2QZ

ISBN: 978-1-83996-054-3

CONTENTS

Features in this exam kit

In addition to providing a wide ranging bank of real exam style questions, we have also included in this kit:

- unit-specific information and advice on exam technique

- our recommended approach to make your revision for this particular unit as effective as possible.

You will find a wealth of other resources to help you with your studies on the AAT website:

www.aat.org.uk/

Quality and accuracy are of the utmost importance to us so if you spot an error in any of our products, please send an email to mykaplanreporting@kaplan.com with full details, or follow the link to the feedback form in MyKaplan.

Our Quality Co-ordinator will work with our technical team to verify the error and take action to ensure it is corrected in future editions.

UNIT-SPECIFIC INFORMATION

THE EXAM

FORMAT OF THE ASSESSMENT

The assessment will comprise eleven independent tasks. Students will be assessed by computer-based assessment.

In any one assessment, students may not be assessed on all content, or on the full depth or breadth of a piece of content. The content assessed may change over time to ensure validity of assessment, but all assessment criteria will be tested over time.

The learning outcomes for this unit are as follows:

	Learning outcome	Weighting
1	Understand how to set up bookkeeping systems	20%
2	Process customer transactions	20%
3	Process supplier transactions	20%
4	Process receipts and payments	20%
5	Process transactions into the ledger accounts	20%
	Total	**100%**

Time allowed

1 hour and 30 minutes.

PASS MARK

The pass mark for all AAT CBAs is 70%.

 Always keep your eye on the clock and make sure you attempt all questions!

DETAILED SYLLABUS

The detailed syllabus and study guide written by the AAT can be found at:

www.aat.org.uk/

INDEX TO QUESTIONS AND ANSWERS

KAPLAN PUBLISHING

EXAM TECHNIQUE

- **Do not skip any of the material** in the syllabus.

- **Read each question** very carefully.

- **Double-check your answer** before committing yourself to it.

- Answer **every** question – if you do not know an answer to a multiple choice question or true/false question, you don't lose anything by guessing. Think carefully before you **guess**.

- If you are answering a multiple-choice question, **eliminate first those answers that you know are wrong.** Then choose the most appropriate answer from those that are left.

- **Don't panic** if you realise you've answered a question incorrectly. Getting one question wrong will not mean the difference between passing and failing.

Computer-based exams – tips

- Do not attempt a CBA until you have **completed all study material** relating to it.

- On the AAT website there is a CBA demonstration. It is **ESSENTIAL** that you attempt this before your real CBA. You will become familiar with how to move around the CBA screens and the way that questions are formatted, increasing your confidence and speed in the actual exam.

- Be sure you understand how to use the **software** before you start the exam. If in doubt, ask the assessment centre staff to explain it to you.

- Questions are **displayed on the screen** and answers are entered using keyboard and mouse. At the end of the exam, you are given a certificate showing the result you have achieved.

- In addition to the traditional multiple-choice question type, CBAs will also contain **other types of questions**, such as number entry questions, drag and drop, true/false, pick lists or drop down menus or hybrids of these.

- In some CBAs you will have to type in complete computations or written answers.

- You need to be sure you **know how to answer questions** of this type before you sit the exam, through practice.

KAPLAN'S RECOMMENDED REVISION APPROACH

QUESTION PRACTICE IS THE KEY TO SUCCESS

Success in professional examinations relies upon you acquiring a firm grasp of the required knowledge at the tuition phase. In order to be able to do the questions, knowledge is essential.

However, the difference between success and failure often hinges on your exam technique on the day and making the most of the revision phase of your studies.

The **Kaplan Study Text** is the starting point, designed to provide the underpinning knowledge to tackle all questions. However, in the revision phase, poring over text books is not the answer.

Kaplan Pocket Notes are designed to help you quickly revise a topic area; however you then need to practise questions. There is a need to progress to exam style questions as soon as possible, and to tie your exam technique and technical knowledge together.

The importance of question practice cannot be over-emphasised.

The recommended approach below is designed by expert tutors in the field, in conjunction with their knowledge of the examiner and the specimen assessment.

You need to practise as many questions as possible in the time you have left.

OUR AIM

Our aim is to get you to the stage where you can attempt exam questions confidently, to time, in a closed book environment, with no supplementary help (i.e. to simulate the real examination experience).

Practising your exam technique is also vitally important for you to assess your progress and identify areas of weakness that may need more attention in the final run up to the examination.

In order to achieve this we recognise that initially you may feel the need to practice some questions with open book help.

Good exam technique is vital.

KAPLAN PUBLISHING

THE KAPLAN REVISION PLAN

Stage 1: Assess areas of strengths and weaknesses

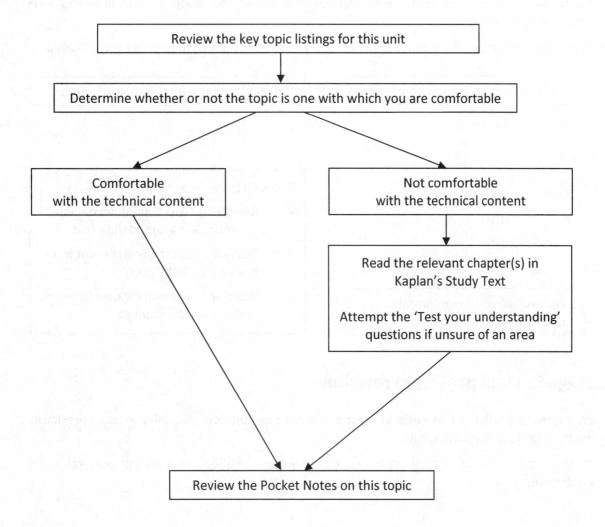

Stage 2: Practice questions

Follow the order of revision of topics as presented in this Kit and attempt the questions in the order suggested.

Try to avoid referring to Study Texts and your notes and the model answer until you have completed your attempt.

Review your attempt with the model answer and assess how much of the answer you achieved.

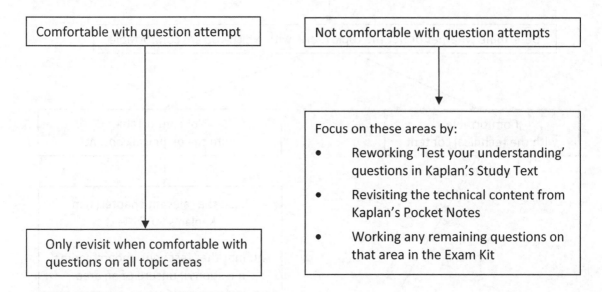

| Comfortable with question attempt | Not comfortable with question attempts |

Focus on these areas by:

- Reworking 'Test your understanding' questions in Kaplan's Study Text
- Revisiting the technical content from Kaplan's Pocket Notes
- Working any remaining questions on that area in the Exam Kit

Only revisit when comfortable with questions on all topic areas

Stage 3: Final pre-exam revision

We recommend that you **attempt at least one mock examination** containing a set of previously unseen exam-standard questions.

Attempt the mock CBA online in timed, closed book conditions to simulate the real exam experience.

Section 1

PRACTICE QUESTIONS

UNDERSTAND HOW TO SET UP BOOKKEEPING SYSTEMS

1   LEO LTD

Leo Ltd codes all sales invoices with a customer code AND a general ledger code. A selection of the codes used is given below.

Customer	Customer account code
DEF Ltd	DEF14
Gamma Production	GAM27
MBG Co	MBG20
Harley Interiors	HAR18
Clarkson Wholesale	CLA16

Item	General ledger code
Standard bath	GL529
Standard washbasin	GL526
Luxury taps	GL530
Bathroom cabinet	GL521
Toilet	GL535
Standard light switch	GL528

Leo Ltd	
121 Apple Lane	
Cuddington, CU9 8EF	
VAT Registration No. 398 2774 01	

DEF Ltd	
51 Neville Street,	18 Aug 20XX
Manchester, M1 4PJ	
10 .... Luxury taps for washbasin @ £8.80 each	£88.00
VAT	£17.60
Total	£105.60

(a) **Select which codes would be used to code this invoice.**

General ledger code	Picklist: DEF14, GL529, GAM27, GL 526, GL530, GL521, GL535, CLA16
Customer account code	Picklist: GL530, GL526, DEF14, MBG20, HAR18, GL521, GL528, GAM27

(b) **Why is it useful to use a customer code?**

Picklist: To help when inventory (stock) taking

To help when completing a tax return

To help find the total amount due to a supplier

To help trace orders and amounts due from particular customers

2   ELLA'S PAINTS

Ella's Paint's codes all purchases invoices with a supplier code AND a general ledger code. A selection of the codes used is given below.

Supplier	Supplier account code
Peak Ltd	PEA27
Marker Production	MAR19
MEG & Co	MEG20
Farley Interiors	FAR12
Hammond Wholesale	HAM16

Item	General ledger code
White Paint	GL360
Standard Roller	GL395
Standard Brush	GL320
Yellow Paint	GL370
Roller tray	GL330

This is an invoice received from a supplier.

Meg & Co
12 Barker Street
Leeds L1 4NZ
VAT Registration No. 402 2958 02

Ella's Paints	
19 Edmund St,	18 Feb 20XX
Newcastle, NE6 5DJ	
20 .... standard rollers @ £2.30 each	£46.00
VAT	£9.20
Total	£55.20

(a)   **Select which codes would be used to code this invoice.**

General ledger code	Picklist: PEA27, MAR19, GL360, MEG20, GL395, FAR12, GL330, HAM 16
Supplier account code	Picklist: PEA27, MAR19, GL360, MEG20, GL395, FAR12, GL330, HAM 16

(b)   **Why is it useful to use a supplier code?**

Picklist: To help when inventory (stock) taking

To help when completing a tax return

To help trace orders and amounts due to particular suppliers

To help trace orders and amounts due from particular customers

3   ROBERTO & CO

Roberto & Co codes all purchase invoices with a supplier code AND a general ledger code. A selection of the codes used is given below.

Supplier	Supplier account code
Alex Ltd	ALE1
Toyworld	TOY10
Pudding and Co	PUD4
Springclean Ltd	SPR7
Spoonaway	SPO3

Item	General ledger code
Food	GL18
Toys	GL72
Stationery	GL45
Cleaning Equipment	GL78
Kitchenware	GL29

This is an invoice received from a supplier.

Alex Ltd
Cherry Way, Haworth, BD22 9HQ
VAT Registration No. 248 2764 00

Roberto & Co	
Roberto House	
Ashton, AS2 8TN	1 Jan 20XX
10 .... teddy bears @ £4 each	£40.00
VAT	£8.00
Total	£48.00

(a)   **Select which codes would be used to code this invoice.**

Supplier account code	Picklist: ALE1, TOY10, PUD4, SPR7, SPO3, GL18, GL72, GL45, GL78, GL29
General ledger code	Picklist: ALE1, TOY10, PUD4, SPR7, SPO3, GL18, GL72, GL45, GL78, GL29

(b) **Why is it necessary to use a general ledger code?**

Picklist: To help when filling in a VAT return

To help when bar coding an item of inventory

To help find the total amount owing to a supplier

To help calculate expense incurred in a GL account

4 ACCOUNTING EQUATION 1

Financial accounting is based upon the accounting equation.

(a) **Show whether the following statements are true or false.**

Item	True/False
Assets less capital is equal to liabilities	
Assets plus liabilities are equal to capital	
Capital plus liabilities are equal to assets	

(b) **Classify each of the following items as an asset or a liability.**

Item	Asset or liability?
Inventory	
Machinery	
5 year loan	

5 CLASSIFICATION

Classify each of the accounts below by adjoining a line between the account and correct classification.

Accounts	Classification
Payables (PLCA)	Asset
Inventory	Income
Commission received	Liability

6   ACCOUNTING EQUATION 2

Financial accounting is based upon the accounting equation.

(a)   Show whether the following statements are true or false.

Item	True/False
Capital is equal to assets plus liabilities	
Assets less liabilities are equal to capital	
Liabilities are equal to capital plus assets	

(b)   Classify each of the following items as an asset or a liability.

Item	Asset or liability?
VAT owed to tax authorities	
Amounts owing to payables	
Money in the bank	

7   CAPEX

It is important to understand the difference between capital expenditure, revenue expenditure, capital income and revenue income.

Select one option in each instance below to show whether the item will be capital income, revenue income, capital expenditure or revenue expenditure.

Item	Capital income	Revenue income	Capital expenditure	Revenue expenditure
Receipt from sale of motor vehicle				
Receipts from credit sales				
Purchase of machinery				
Payment of electricity bill				
Purchase of goods for resale				

8   REVEX

It is important to understand the difference between capital expenditure, revenue expenditure, capital income and revenue income.

Select one option in each instance below to show whether the item will be capital income, revenue income, capital expenditure or revenue expenditure.

Item	Capital income	Revenue income	Capital expenditure	Revenue expenditure
Receipt from sale of machinery				
Payment of telephone bill				
Purchase of building				
Receipts from cash sales				
Receipts from receivables				

9   EXPENDITURE TYPES

It is important to understand the difference between capital expenditure, revenue expenditure, capital income and revenue income.

Select one option in each instance below to show whether the item will be capital expenditure, revenue expenditure, capital income or revenue income.

Item	Capital expenditure	Revenue expenditure	Capital income	Revenue income
Purchase of a new computer system				
Receipts from customers				
Receipt from sale of fixtures and fittings				
Payments of salaries to staff				
Purchase of cleaning materials				
Receipt of bank interest				

10   ASSET OR LIABILITY

(a)   **Classify each of the following items as an asset or a liability.**

Item	Asset or liability?
Factory building	
Money due to suppliers	
Car used in the business	

ABC Co has paid an electricity bill by cheque.

(b)   **Complete the sentence below by selecting the correct option to show how this transaction will affect the accounts of ABC Co.**

The expense electricity will **increase/decrease**; the asset of bank will **increase/decrease**.

11   ACCOUNTING EQUATION 3

Show the accounting equation by inserting the appropriate figures using the information provided below:

Note: All figures should be shown as a positive balance.

Assets and liabilities	£
Land & buildings	120,000
Cars & machinery	20,960
Amounts due from credit customers	4,900
Bank	12,500
Amounts due to credit suppliers	13,870
Loan	15,000

Assets £	Liabilities £	Capital £

12   MULTIPLE CHOICE 1

(a)   **State whether each of the following costs should be treated as capital expenditure or revenue expense.**

		Capital expenditure or revenue expense
(i)	Work to install additional, high-specification, electrical power cabling and circuits so that additional plant and equipment can become operational	
(ii)	Replacement of some loose and damaged roof tiles following a recent storm	
(iii)	Repainting the factory administration office	
(iv)	Modifications to the factory entrance to enable a large item of plant and equipment to be installed	

(b) **Which of the following statements best defines a statement of financial position?**

A   It is a summary of income and expenditure for an accounting period

B   It is a summary of cash receipts and payments made during an accounting period

C   It is a summary of assets, liabilities and equity at a specified date

D   It is a summary of assets and expenses at a specified date

(c) **The double-entry system of bookkeeping normally results in which of the following balances on the ledger accounts?**

	Debit balances:	Credit balances:
A	Assets and revenues	Liabilities, capital and expenses
B	Revenues, capital and liabilities	Assets and expenses
C	Assets and expenses	Liabilities, capital and revenues
D	Assets, expenses and capital	Liabilities and revenues

13 MULTIPLE CHOICE 2

(a) **Which of the following statements best defines a statement of profit or loss?**

A   It is a summary of assets and expenses at a specified date

B   It is a summary of cash receipts and payments made during an accounting period

C   It is a summary of assets, liabilities and equity at a specified date

D   It is a summary of income and expenditure for an accounting period

(b) **Which one of the following statements is correct?**

A   Assets and liabilities normally have credit balances

B   Liabilities and revenues normally have debit balances

C   Assets and revenues normally have credit balances

D   Assets and expenses normally have debit balances

(c) **Which one of the following statements is not correct?**

A   A credit balance exists where the total of credit entries is more than the total of debit entries

B   A debit balance exists where the total of debit entries is less than the total of credit entries

C   A credit balance exists where the total of debit entries is less than the total of credit entries

D   A debit balance exists where the total of debit entries is more than the total of credit entries

14 LEO

(a) Given below are a number of Leo's transactions. For each transaction, tick the relevant box to indicate whether it is a cash transaction or a credit transaction.

TRANSACTION		CASH	CREDIT
(i)	Receipt of goods worth £140.59 from a supplier together with an invoice for that amount.		
(ii)	Payment of £278.50 by cheque for a purchase at the till.		
(iii)	Receipt of a deposit of £15.00 for goods.		
(iv)	Sending of an invoice for £135.00 to the payer of the deposit for the remaining value of the goods.		
(v)	Sale of goods for £14.83, payment received by credit card.		

(b) Given below are a number of typical transactions and balances that might be found in a business such as that run by Leo. Fill in the boxes to indicate whether the items are assets, liabilities, expenses or income.

(i)	Goods stored in the warehouse awaiting resale	
(ii)	Electricity bill paid	
(iii)	Sale of goods	
(iv)	Amounts owing from a customer	
(v)	Rent paid for the factory building	
(vi)	Amounts due to the owner	
(vii)	Amounts owed to suppliers	
(viii)	Cash held in the till	
(ix)	Machinery purchased for use in the factory	
(x)	Rent received for subletting part of the factory premises	
(xi)	Cash held in the business bank account	

15   ACCOUNT CODES

This task is about manual and digital bookkeeping systems.

Accounts need to be created for a new customer and a new supplier. Account codes follow the format shown below:

A letter C to indicate a customer account, or a letter S to indicate a supplier account.

The first 4 digits of the customer or suppliers name.

A 3 digit sequential number representing the number of customer or supplier accounts.

(a)   **Enter the account codes for the new customer and new supplier.**

Date	Customer name	Customer account code
1 August	Worthington Ltd	CWORT092
4 August	Moss Plc	

Date	Supplier name	Supplier account code
2 August	Morley & Sons	SMORL076
5 August	Chapman Ltd	

(b)   **Identify whether the following statements regarding digital bookkeeping systems are true or false.**

Statement	True ✓	False ✓
The reconciliation between the individual payables ledger and the control account is completed automatically		
General ledger accounts need to be manually balanced off to extract a trial balance		

(c)   **A sales invoice for a credit customer has been entered as a sales credit note incorrectly in the digital bookkeeping system. Identify TWO consequences of this error.**

Consequence	✓
The total sales value will be understated	
The business may despatch goods that have not been sold	
The total amount owed to payables will be understated	
The business may be paid for goods that have not been sold	
The business may pay the incorrect amount to a supplier	
The business will receive more money from a customer than they are expecting per their customer report	

(d) **Identify which document or statement would be used for each of the purposes below.**

Summarising the transactions for a period and classifying them into relevant categories of income and expenditure to show the overall profit or loss for the period	
Detailing all of the transactions with a credit customer during the period and advising a credit customer of the balance outstanding on their account	
To summarise the balances on each of the general ledger accounts in order to begin the preparation of the financial statements	
To correct an invoice that has been prepared incorrectly by overstating the value of goods supplied	

Options
Petty cash voucher
Trial balance
Statement of profit or loss
Bank statement
Invoice
Supplier statement
Credit note

16 PRINCIPLES 1

This task is about the principles of double entry bookkeeping.

At the end of the accounting period, a business had the following assets and liabilities.

Assets and liabilities	£
Motor vehicles	10,180.00
Cash at bank	4,367.45
Inventory	2,100.00
Receivables	4,589.45
Payables	8,392.48
Bank overdraft	1,536.97

(a) **Complete the table below showing the accounting equation.**

Assets £	Liabilities £	Capital £

The following business transactions have taken place:

Purchased a van for use in the business and agreed to pay the supplier at a later date.

Sold some goods to a customer for cash, making a profit on the sale.

(b) **Identify the dual effect of these transactions, by selecting the correct options for each transaction below.**

Transaction 1	
Effect	✓
Increase assets	
Decrease assets	
Increase capital	
Increase liabilities	
Decrease liabilities	

Transaction 2	
Effect	✓
Increase liabilities	
Increase capital	
Decrease capital	
Increase assets	
Decrease liabilities	

A trial balance has been extracted from a business' bookkeeping system.

(c) **Identify which side of the trial balance the following account balances would appear.**

Account balance	Debit ✓	Credit ✓
Opening inventory		
Payables		
Drawings		

17 DIGITAL BOOKKEEPING

This task is about manual and digital bookkeeping systems.

A business has started to sell a new type of product, and therefore additional general ledger codes need to be created in the digital bookkeeping system. All general ledger codes are 4 digits, and follow the format below:

- Asset codes start 0, followed by a 3 digit sequential code that represents the number of asset codes

- Liability codes start 1, followed by a 3 digit sequential code that represents the number of liability codes

- Income codes start 2, followed by a 3 digit sequential code that represents the number of income codes

- Expense codes start 3, followed by a 3 digit sequential code that represents the number of expense codes

(a) **Enter the account codes for each of the new general ledger codes below.**

Details	Ledger code		Details	Ledger code
Sales – dog food	2019		Insurance expense	3072
Sales – dog bedding			Courier expense	
Sales – dog toys			Advertising expense	

(b)   **Identify the coding system used in the general ledger.**

Coding system	✓
Alphanumerical	
Alphabetical	
Numerical	

An invoice for the purchase of a motor vehicle for use within the business has been entered as motor expenses in the general ledger.

(c)   **Identify TWO consequences of this error.**

Consequence	✓
Assets will be understated	
Sales will be understated	
Purchases will be understated	
Expenses will be overstated	

(d)   **Identify whether the following statements about digital bookkeeping are true or false.**

Statement	True ✓	False ✓
It is not possible to post a duplicate transaction using a digital bookkeeping system		
Digital bookkeeping systems can automatically post recurring entries		
The trial balance will automatically balance using a digital bookkeeping system		

18   PRINCIPLES 2

This task is about the principles of double entry bookkeeping.

(a)   **Classify the following items by choosing from the available options (you may use each option more than once).**

Item	
Motor vehicles	
Insurance costs	
Drawings	
Payables	

Options
Assets
Liabilities
Income
Expenses
Capital

The transactions shown below have taken place and been entered into the general ledger.

(b) **Identify the opposite effect of each transaction. You should ignore VAT.**

Transaction	Dual effect 1	Dual effect 2
Owner invests £20,000 cash into the business bank account	Increases assets	
Purchases a laptop computer for use within the business, paying in cash	Increases assets	
Makes a sale to a customer realising a profit on the sale. Customer agrees to pay at a later date	Increases capital	
Owner withdraws £10,000 cash from the business to pay for a private holiday	Decreases assets	
A credit customer pays the amount owed	Increases assets	

Options
Increases assets
Decreases assets
Increases liabilities
Decreases liabilities
Increases capital
Decreases capital

At the end of the accounting period, a business has the following account balances:

Item	Balance £
Office equipment	Unknown
Receivables	4,593.90
Cash	1,342.80
Bank loan	6,780.00
Inventory	1,030.00
Capital	3,486.70

(c) **Use the accounting equation to calculate the office equipment balance.**

£	

19   PRINCIPLES 3

(a)   It is important to understand the difference between capital expenditure, revenue expenditure, capital income and revenue income.

Select one option in each instance below to show whether the item will be capital expenditure, revenue expenditure, capital income or revenue income.

Item	Capital expenditure	Revenue expenditure	Capital income	Revenue income
Purchase of computer equipment				
Receipts from credit sales				
Receipt from sale of motor vehicle (non-current asset)				
Purchase of motor vehicle				
Purchase of stationery				
Payment of rent				

(b)   **Show whether the following statements are true or false.**

Statement	True ✓	False ✓
Assets less liabilities are equal to capital		
The business and owner are treated as two separate entities		
A debit increases an item of income		

(c)   **Classify each of the following items as an asset or a liability.**

Item	Option	Options
Computer equipment		Assets
Petty cash		Liabilities
Money owed to suppliers		

PROCESS CUSTOMER TRANSACTIONS

20 ALESSANDRO LTD

On 1 August Alessandro Ltd delivered the following goods to a credit customer, Palermo Wholesale.

Alessandro Ltd
8 Alan Street
Glasgow, G1 7DJ

Delivery note No. 24369
01 Aug 20XX

Palermo Wholesale   **Customer account code:** AGG42
17 Zoo Lane
Dartford
DH8 4TJ

40 standard baths, product code SB05

The list price of the goods was £62.50 each plus VAT. Palermo Wholesale are to be given a 12% trade discount and a 5% discount if they pay within 5 working days.

(a) **Complete the invoice below.**

Alessandro Ltd
8 Alan Street
Glasgow, G1 7DJ
VAT Registration No. 398 2774 01

Palermo Wholesale   **Customer account code:**
167 Front St
Stanley
DH8 4TJ   **Delivery note number:**
                                     Date: 1 Aug 20XX
Invoice No: 327

Quantity	Product code	Total list price £	Net amount after discount £	VAT £	Gross £

Alessandro Ltd offers each customer a discount of 5% if they pay within 30 days.

(b) **What is the name of this type of discount?**

Picklist: Bulk discount, prompt payment discount, trade discount

---

21 HLB WHOLESALE

On 1 February Painting Supplies Ltd delivered the following goods to a credit customer, HLB Wholesale.

Painting Supplies Ltd
19 Edmund St
Newcastle, NE6 5DJ

Delivery note No. 46589

01 Feb 20XX

HLB Wholesale   **Customer account code:** HLB24

98 Back St

Consett

DH4 3PD

20 tins of white paint, product code SD19

The list price of the goods was £15 each plus VAT. HLB Wholesale are to be given a 10% trade discount and a 4% discount if they pay within 4 working days.

(a) Complete the invoice below.

Painting Supplies Ltd
19 Edmund St
Newcastle, NE6 5DJ

VAT Registration No. 402 2958 02

HLB Wholesale   **Customer account code:**
98 Back St
Consett
DH4 3PD   **Delivery note number:**

Date: 1 Feb 20XX   **Invoice No:** 298

Quantity	Product code	Total list price £	Net amount after discount £	VAT £	Gross £

Painting Supplies Ltd offer a discount of 10% if their customers buy from them.

(b) What is the name of this type of discount?

[   ]

Picklist: Bulk discount, prompt payment discount, trade discount

22   MASHED LTD

On 1 August Hickory House delivered the following goods to a credit customer, Mashed Ltd.

Hickory House
22 Nursery Road
Keighley, BD22 7BD

Delivery note No. 472
01 Aug 20XX

Mashed Ltd   **Customer account code:** MA87
42 Moorside Court
Ilkley
Leeds, LS29 4PR

20 flower pots, product code P10

The list price of the goods was £5 per flower pot plus VAT. Mashed Ltd is to be given a 10% trade discount and a 4% early payment discount.

(a)   Complete the invoice below.

Hickory House
22 Nursery Road
Keighley, BD22 7BD

VAT Registration No. 476 1397 02

Mashed Ltd   **Customer account code:**
42 Moorside Court
Ilkley   **Delivery note number:**
Leeds, LS29 4PR

                                                    Date: 1 Aug 20XX
Invoice No: 47

Quantity of pots	Product code	Total list price £	Net amount after discount £	VAT £	Gross £

Hickory House offers each customer a discount if they buy over a certain quantity of goods.

(b)   What is the name of this type of discount?

[   ]

Picklist: Bulk discount, prompt payment discount, trade discount

23   ROCKY RICARDO

On 1 December Rocky Ricardo delivered the following goods to a credit customer, Alpha Group.

**Rocky Ricardo
1 Rocky Way
Middleton, M42 5TU**

Delivery note No. 2132
01 Dec 20XX

Alpha Group   **Customer account code:** ALP01
Alpha House
Warwick
WR11 5TB

200 cases of product A, product code A1.

The list price of the goods was £10 per case plus VAT. Alpha Group are to be given a 10% trade discount and a 2% prompt payment discount.

(a)   Complete the invoice below.

Rocky Ricardo

1 Rocky Way

Middleton, M42 5TU

VAT Registration No. 298 3827 04

Alpha Group   Customer account code:

Alpha House

Warwick   Delivery note number:

WR11 5TB

                                             Date: 1 Dec 20XX

Invoice No: 950

Quantity of cases	Product code	Total list price £	Net amount after discount £	VAT £	Gross £

(b)   What will be the amounts entered into the sales daybook after the invoice in (a) has been prepared?

Sales daybook					
Date 20XX	**Details**	**Invoice No:**	**Total £**	**VAT £**	**Net £**
1 Dec	Alpha Group	950			

A cheque for £1,000 has now been received from Alpha Group which incorrectly states is full settlement of their account. Their account in the receivables ledger is shown below:

Alpha Group

Date 20XX	Details	Amount £	Date 20XX	Details	Amount £
1 Oct	Balance b/f	4,288	3 Oct	Bank	4,288
21 Nov	Invoice 123	1,500	25 Nov	Credit note 102	500
29 Nov	Invoice 189	2,000			

(c)   **Which item has not been included in the payment?**

[ ]

Select your account name from the following list: Balance b/f, Invoice 123, Invoice 189, Bank, Credit note 102

(d)   An invoice has been sent to Alpha Group for £500 plus VAT of £100. A prompt payment discount of 1% has been offered for payment within 5 days.

(i)   **What is the amount Alpha Group should pay if payment is made within 5 days?**

£ [ ]

(ii)   **What is the amount Alpha Group should pay if payment is NOT made within 5 days?**

£ [ ]

24   SDB

Sales invoices have been prepared and partially entered in the sales daybook, as shown below.

(a)   **Complete the entries in the sales daybook by inserting the appropriate figures for each invoice.**

(b)   **Total the last five columns of the sales daybook.**

Sales daybook

Date 20XX	Details	Invoice number	Total £	VAT £	Net £	Sales type 1 £	Sales type 2 £
31 Dec	Poonams	105	3,600				3,000
31 Dec	D. Taylor	106		1,280		6,400	
31 Dec	Smiths	107	3,840		3,200		3,200
	Totals						

25 MAHINDRA LTD

Sales invoices have been received and partially entered in the sales daybook of Mahindra Ltd, as shown below.

(a) **Complete the entries in the sales daybook by inserting the appropriate figures for each invoice.**

(b) **Total the last five columns of the sales daybook.**

Sales daybook

Date 20XX	Details	Invoice number	Total £	VAT £	Net £	Sales type 1 £	Sales type 2 £
31 Jan	Square Ltd	3567			1,000	1,000	
31 Jan	Oval & Co	3568		1,600			8,000
31 Jan	Diamond Ltd	3569	13,200				11,000
31 Jan	Triangle Ltd	3570		1,320		6,600	
	Totals						

26 PAR FOR THE COURSE GOLF SUPPLIES

Customer invoice number 2808 is being prepared based on the following customer quotation.

> Par for the Course Golf Supplies Ltd
>
> To: Erehwon Golf Club   Date: 13 August 20XX
>
> Customer code: EREH094
>
> Further to your enquiry, we are pleased to provide a quotation for the supply of:
>
> 300 units of product 107:
>
> Pack of 12 golf balls @ £5.40 each (discounted to £5.00 each for purchases of 250 units or more)
>
> 150 units of product 119:   Golf umbrellas @ £7.90 each
>
> Plus VAT at 20%
>
> Payment terms: 30 days from end of month of invoice.

(a) **Identify which type of discount was offered to the customer.**

Discount type	✓
Prompt payment	
Trade	
Bulk	

(b) **Calculate the amounts to include on the customer invoice.**

	£
Net amount after discounts	
VAT @ 20%	
Total	

(c) **Enter the invoice into the digital bookkeeping system by selecting the correct menu option, and making the necessary accounting entries.**

Menu option	✓
Purchases daybook	
Purchase returns daybook	
Cash book	
Sales daybook	
Sales returns daybook	
Discounts allowed daybook	
Discounts received daybook	

Date	Customer code	Customer	General ledger code	Invoice number	Net £	VAT code
13 Aug		Erehwon Golf Club	Option 1			Option 2

Option 1	✓
1001 Sales – golf equipment	
1002 Sales – golf buggies	
4001 Purchases – golf equipment	
7001 Receivables	

Option 2	✓
V0 – 0%	
V5 – 5%	
V20 – 20%	

27   LINKEES TOY MAKERS LTD

Customer invoice number 2808 is being prepared based on the following customer quotation.

Linkees Toy Makers Ltd
To: Thomas' Toys   Date: 17 May 20XX
Customer code: THOM08
Further to your enquiry, we are pleased to provide a quotation for the supply of:
150 units of product B64: Board games (assorted) @ £4.50 each
Plus VAT at 20%
Payment terms: 30 days from end of month of invoice. 5% discount if payment received within 14 days from date of invoice.

(a)   **Identify which type of discount has been offered to the customer.**

Discount type	✓
Prompt payment	
Trade	
Bulk	

(b)   **Calculate the amounts to include on the customer invoice.**

	£
Net amount after discounts	
VAT @ 20%	
Total	

(c)   **Enter the invoice into the digital bookkeeping system by selecting the correct menu option, and making the necessary entries.**

Menu option	✓
Purchases daybook	
Purchase returns daybook	
Cash book	
Sales daybook	
Sales returns daybook	
Discounts allowed daybook	
Discounts received daybook	

Date	Customer code	Customer	General ledger code	Invoice number	Net £	VAT code
17 May		Thomas' Toys	Option 1			Option 2

Option 1	✓
1001 Sales – toys	
1002 Sales – board games	
4001 Purchases – Inventory	
7001 Receivables	

Option 2	✓
V0 – 0%	
V5 – 5%	
V20 – 20%	
V1 – Exempt	

28 WILLIAM & SAMMY LTD

The account shown below is in the receivables ledger of Hickory House. A cheque for £668 has now been received from this customer.

William and Sammy Ltd

Date 20XX	Details	Amount £	Date 20XX	Details	Amount £
1 June	Balance b/f	4,250	2 June	Bank	4,250
23 June	Sales invoice 255	1,876	15 June	Sales returns credit note 98	1,208
30 June	Sales Invoice 286	2,459			

(a) **Which item has not been included in the payment?**

Picklist: Balance b/f, Sales invoice 255, Sales invoice 286, Bank, Sales returns credit note 98

An invoice is being prepared to be sent to William and Sammy Ltd for £3,890 plus VAT of £778. A prompt payment discount of 4% will be offered for payment within 10 days.

(b) **What is the amount Hickory House should receive if payment is made within 10 days?**

£

(c) **What is the amount Hickory House should receive if payment is NOT made within 10 days?**

£

29   DIAMONDS & RUBIES LTD

The following is a summary of transactions with Diamonds & Rubies Ltd, a new credit customer.

Invoice 3927, 5 August, £4,640
Credit note 96, 10 August, £980
Invoice 3964, 21 August, £1,560
Credit note 104, 28 August, £650
Cheque received, 30 August, £2,100

Complete the statement of account below.

Stavros

121 Baker St

Newcastle, NE1 7DJ

To: Diamonds & Rubies Ltd   **Date:** 31 Aug 20XX

Date 20XX	Details	Transaction amount £	Outstanding amount £
5 Aug	Invoice 3927		
10 Aug	Credit note 96		
21 Aug	Invoice 3964		
28 Aug	Credit note 104		
30 Aug	Cheque received		

30   MAX LTD

The following is a summary of transactions with Max Ltd, a new credit customer of Painting Supplies Ltd.

Invoice 4658, 5 Feb. £2,560
Invoice 3964, 11 Feb, £3,290
Credit note 125, 21 Feb, £230
Credit note 139, 23 Feb, £560
Cheque received, 27 Feb, £1,900

Complete the statement of account below.

		Painting Supplies Ltd	
		19 Edmund St	
		Newcastle, NE6 5DJ	

To: Max Ltd — **Date:** 28 Feb 20XX

Date 20XX	Details	Transaction amount £	Outstanding amount £
5 Feb	Invoice 4658		
11 Feb	Invoice 3964		
21 Feb	Credit note 125		
23 Feb	Credit note 139		
27 Feb	Cheque received		

31   BETA BOARDS

The following is a summary of transactions with Ava Ltd, a new credit customer of Beta Boards

£350 re invoice 222 of 10 Aug
Cheque for £225 received 12 Aug
£744 re invoice 305 of 15 Aug
£339 re credit note 194 on 20 Aug
Cheque for £530 received 24 Aug

Complete the statement of account below.

		Beta Boards	
		3 Victoria Avenue	
		Troon	
		KA5 2BD	

To: Ava Ltd — **Date:** 31 Aug 20XX

Date 20XX	Details	Transaction amount £	Outstanding amount £
10 Aug	Invoice 222		
12 Aug	Cheque		
15 Aug	Invoice 305		
20 Aug	Credit note 194		
24 Aug	Cheque		

32   BELLA PUMPKIN

The following is a summary of transactions up to 31 December 20XX for Bella Pumpkin, a new credit customer of Rocky Ricardo.

£1,700 re invoice 1001 of 12 December

£2,350 re invoice 1004 of 21 December

£940 re credit note 101 of 21 December

£470 re invoice 1010 of 27 December

Cheque for £2,000 received 29 December

(a)   Enter the transactions into the receivables ledger of Bella Pumpkin.

(b)   Insert the balance carried down and the balance brought down together with date and details.

Bella Pumpkin

Date 20XX	Details	Amount £	Date 20XX	Details	Amount £

(c)   Complete the statement of account below to be sent to Bella Pumpkin

<table>
<tr><td colspan="4" align="center">Rocky Ricardo
1 Rocky Way
Middleton, M42 5TU</td></tr>
<tr><td colspan="2">To: Bella Pumpkin</td><td colspan="2">Date: 31 Dec 20XX</td></tr>
<tr><td>Date 20XX</td><td>Details</td><td align="center">Transaction amount
£</td><td align="center">Outstanding amount
£</td></tr>
<tr><td></td><td></td><td></td><td></td></tr>
<tr><td></td><td></td><td></td><td></td></tr>
<tr><td></td><td></td><td></td><td></td></tr>
<tr><td></td><td></td><td></td><td></td></tr>
<tr><td></td><td></td><td></td><td></td></tr>
</table>

33 HENRY LTD

Henry Ltd received two cheques from William & Co totalling £3,361.26, as detailed in the remittance advices below. The customer has been offered a prompt payment discount of 5% for payment within 10 days.

William & Co Remittance advice 3671 16 Aug 20XX	
Invoice	£
1028	473.87
1046	1,006.62
1059	462.20
Total	1,942.69

William & Co Remittance advice 3684 22 Aug 20XX	
Invoice	£
1068	789.48
1096	629.09
Total	1,418.57

Company policy is to match each transaction with the remittance advice number to query any under or overpayment.

(a) **Allocate the amounts received by identifying the appropriate action in the customer report below. You may use each action more than once.**

Transaction type	Date	Details	Amount £	Action
Balance b/f	1 Aug 20XX		473.87	
Invoice 1046	4 Aug 20XX	Goods	1,059.60	
Invoice 1059	9 Aug 20XX	Services	462.20	
Credit note CN108	9 Aug 20XX	Correction – Invoice 1046	52.98	
Invoice 1068	10 Aug 20XX	Goods	789.48	
Invoice 1096	14 Aug 20XX	Goods	662.20	

Action
Allocate full amount – 1028
Query underpayment
Allocate full amount – 1059
Query overpayment
Allocate full amount – 1096
Allocate full amount – 1056
Allocate full amount – 1068

Trinity Pet Products have a policy of offering customers a 5% prompt payment discount for payment within 10 days of the invoice date.

(b)   Complete the table below by calculating the amount that **Trinity Pet Products should receive, assuming both customers take advantage of the prompt payment discount offered.**

Customer name	Invoice number	Amount before discount £	Amount after prompt payment discount £
Oliver John & Co	387	8,345.60	
Excelsior Ltd	395	4,562.40	

Trinity Pet Products received a payment from another customer qualifying for a prompt payment discount. However, the prompt payment discount has been calculated incorrectly resulting in an underpayment.

(c)   Complete the table below by calculating the amount that should have been paid and the amount that remains outstanding.

Customer name	Prompt payment Discount %	Invoice amount £	Amount paid £	Amount that should have been paid £	Amount outstanding £
Galahad	5	7,529.40	7,093.52		

34   KLOPP & CO

Jurgen Ltd has received two cheques from Klopp & Co totalling £4,273.80, as detailed in the remittance advices below. The customer has been offered a prompt payment discount of 4% for payment within 7 days.

Klopp & Co Remittance advice 2976 17 Apr 20XX	
Invoice	£
Invoice 342	752.34
Invoice 354	475.61
Invoice 362	800.88
Invoice 371	235.68
Total	2,264.51

Klopp & Co Remittance advice 3018 24 Apr 20XX	
Invoice	£
Invoice 379	872.62
Invoice 383	649.23
Invoice 391	487.44
Total	2,009.29

Company policy is to match each transaction with the remittance advice number to query any under or overpayment.

(a) **Allocate the amounts received by identifying the appropriate action in the customer report below. You may use each action more than once.**

Transaction type	Date	Details	Amount £	Action
Balance b/f	1 Apr 20XX		752.34	
Invoice 354	2 Apr 20XX	Goods	475.61	
Invoice 362	9 Apr 20XX	Services	834.25	
Invoice 371	12 Apr 20XX	Services	245.50	
Invoice 379	13 Apr 20XX	Goods	1,051.34	
Credit note 46	14 Apr 20XX	Correction – 379	178.72	
Invoice 383	14 Apr 20XX	Goods	649.23	
Invoice 391	19 Apr 20XX	Goods	507.75	

Action
Allocate full amount – 342
Query underpayment
Allocate full amount – 354
Query overpayment
Allocate full amount – 362
Allocate full amount – 371
Allocate full amount – 379
Allocate full amount – CN46
Allocate full amount – 383
Allocate full amount – 391

Henderson & Co has received a payment from a customer in full settlement of their outstanding balance. When Henderson & Co compare the amount received to the amount outstanding on their customer report, there appears to be an underpayment of £117.48.

(b) **Identify which TWO of the following would explain the reason for this underpayment.**

Reason	✓
The customer has taken a prompt payment discount of 6% that they were not entitled to, on an invoice of £1,958 before the discount.	
Henderson & Co have duplicated an invoice in their system for £96.90 plus 20% VAT.	
2 credit notes for £49.71 and £67.77 have been omitted by Henderson & Co.	
The customer has paid for £117.48 of goods that they never received.	

PROCESS SUPPLIER TRANSACTIONS

35 NAN NURSING

A supply of chocolate puddings have been delivered to Nan Nursing by Pudding and Co. The purchase order sent from Nan Nursing, and the invoice from Pudding and Co, are shown below.

Nan Nursing

22 Nursery Road

Keighley, BD22 7BD

Purchase Order No. HH72

To: Pudding and Co

Date: 15 August 20XX

Please supply 50 chocolate puddings product code 742087

Purchase price: £20 per 10, plus VAT

Discount: less 10% trade discount, as agreed.

Pudding and Co

17 Pudding Lane, Bradford, BD19 7HX

VAT Registration No. 234 7654 00

Invoice No. 428

Nan Nursing

22 Nursery Road

Keighley, BD22 7BD

20 August 20XX

50 chocolate puddings product code 742087 @ £2 each	£50
Less Trade Discount	£10
	————
Net	£40
VAT	£ 8
Total	£48

Terms: 30 days net

Check the invoice against the purchase order and answer the following questions.

(a) Has the correct purchase price of the chocolate puddings been charged?   Y / N

(b) Has the correct total discount been calculated?   Y / N

(c) What would be the VAT amount charged if the invoice was correct?   £_____

(d) What would be the total amount charged if the invoice was correct?   £_____

36   **PIXIE PAPER**

A supply of paper has been delivered to Alpha Ltd by Pixie Paper. The purchase order sent from Alpha Ltd, and the invoice from Pixie Paper, are shown below.

Alpha Ltd

121 Baker St

Newcastle, NE1 7DJ

Purchase Order No. PO1792

To: Pixie Paper

Date: 5 Aug 20XX

Please supply 50 boxes of A4 paper product code 16257

Purchase price: £10 per box, plus VAT

Discount: less 10% trade discount, as agreed.

Pixie Paper

24 Eden Terrace, Durham, DH9 7TE

VAT Registration No. 464 392 401

Invoice No. 1679

Alpha Ltd

121 Baker St

Newcastle, NE1 7DJ

9 Aug 20XX

50 boxes of A4 paper, product code 16257 @ £10 each	£500
VAT	£100
Total	£600
Terms: 30 days net	

Check the invoice against the purchase order and answer the following questions.

(a)	Has the correct product been supplied by Pixie Paper?	**Y / N**
(b)	Has the correct net price been calculated?	**Y / N**
(c)	Has the total invoice price been calculated correctly?	**Y / N**
(d)	What would be the VAT amount charged if the invoice was correct?	£_____
(e)	What would be the total amount charged if the invoice was correct?	£_____

37   PAINTS R US

A supply of paint has been delivered to Painting Supplies Ltd by Paints R Us. The purchase order sent from Painting Supplies Ltd, and the invoice from Paints R Us, are shown below.

Painting Supplies Ltd

19 Edmund St

Newcastle, NE6 5DJ

Purchase Order No. PO6548

To: Paints R Us

Date: 5 Feb 20XX

Please supply 20 tins of blue paint, product code 23567

Purchase price: £8 per tin plus VAT

Discount: less 5% prompt payment discount, as agreed.

Paints R Us

19 Valley Gardens, Stanley, DH5 8JJ

VAT Registration No. 421 385 602

Invoice No. 2485

Painting Supplies Ltd

19 Edmund St

Newcastle, NE6 5DJ

10 Feb 20XX

20 tins of blue paint, product code 23567 @ £8 each	£160.00
VAT	£30.00
Total	£190.00
Terms: 30 days net	

Check the invoice against the purchase order and answer the following questions.

(a)   Has the correct product been supplied?   Y / N

(b)   Has the correct net price been calculated?   Y / N

(c)   Has the total invoice price been calculated correctly?   Y / N

(d)   What would be the VAT amount charged if the invoice was correct?   £_____

(e)   What would be the total amount charged if the invoice was correct?   £_____

38   **MT MOTORS**

MT Motors purchased goods costing £500 from Z (before VAT at 20%). Z gave MT Motors a trade discount of 20%.

(a)   **What was the net amount recognised as a purchase expense after the discount?**

   A   £480.00

   B   £400.00

   C   £600.00

   D   £333.33

(b)   **What was the VAT on purchases after trade discount?**

   A   £100.00

   B   £80.00

   C   £20.00

   D   £94.00

  (c) **Which one of the following statements best describes the purpose of a purchase order?**

    A It is issued to a supplier to request supply of goods from them on terms specified within the order.

    B It is issued to a customer to confirm the supply of goods to them on terms specified in the order.

    C It is issued to a supplier as notification of payment.

    D It confirms the price that will be charged by a supplier for goods supplied.

39 ECHO LTD

A supply of cardboard boxes has been delivered to Rocky Ricardo's by Echo Ltd. The purchase order sent from Rocky Ricardo's, and the invoice from Echo Ltd, are shown below.

Rocky Ricardo

1 Rocky Way

Middleton, M42 5TU

Purchase Order No. RR111

To: Echo Ltd

Date: 7 Dec 20XX

Please supply 1,000 widgets product code 243

Purchase price: £1 per widget, plus VAT

Discount: less 10% trade discount, as agreed

Echo Ltd

2 Walford Way, Essex, ES4 4XX

VAT Registration No. 533 8372 12

Invoice No. 123

Rocky Ricardo

1 Rocky Way

Middleton, M42 5TU

10 Dec 20XX

1,000 .... widgets product code 243 @ £1 each	£1,000.00
VAT	£200.00
Total	£1,200.00

Terms: 30 days net

(a) **Check the invoice against the purchase order and answer the following questions.**

Has the correct discount been applied?   Y / N

How much should the trade discount amount be?   £_____

What would be the VAT amount charged if the invoice was correct?   £_____

The following invoice has been received from the credit supplier Messi Brothers.

Messi Brothers

Unit 3 Fothersway Business Park, Newcastle

VAT Registration No. 933 8982 02

Invoice No. 1365

Rocky Ricardo
1 Rocky Way
Middleton, M42 5TU

10 Dec 20XX

500 .... of product code 1872 @ £3.75 each	£1,875.00
VAT	£375.00
Total	£2,250.00

Terms: 30 days net

(b) **What will be the details and amounts entered into the daybook?**

Daybook:					
Date 20XX	Details	Invoice No:	Total £	VAT £	Net £
10 Dec		1365			

40   GORDON'S TRAIN REPAIRS

The supplier credit note below has been received.

Gordon's Train Repairs Ltd	
To: North Enozraw Railway	Date: 14 October 20XX
Credit note number: CN483	£
Correction of invoice no: 1859	476.50
VAT @ 20%	95.30
Total	571.80

(a)   Identify the daybook in which the credit note will be entered.

Daybook	✓
Sales daybook	
Purchases daybook	
Cashbook	
Purchase returns daybook	
Sales returns daybook	
Discounts allowed daybook	

(b)   Complete the daybook by:

• Making FOUR entries to record the credit note

• Totalling the net, VAT and total columns.

Date 20XX	Supplier	Credit note number	Net £	VAT £	Total £
17 May	Narrow Gauge Ltd	CN869	317.60	63.52	381.12
26 June	Island of Sodor plc	CN0289	84.00	16.80	100.80
8 Aug	Topham Hatt & Co	421	98.50	19.70	118.20
13 Sep	Flying Kipper Ltd	C980	206.00	41.20	247.20
14 Oct	Gordon's Train Repairs				
		Totals			

The invoice and goods received note below relate to an incorrect invoice received by North Enozraw Railway.

North Enozraw Railway
Goods received note GRN462
22 January 20XX
Goods received from Ulfstead Ltd:
10 iron girders
Received as ordered
Price per unit : £1,000 + VAT @ 20%

Ulfstead Ltd

To: North Enozraw Railway   Date: 22 Jan 20XX

Invoice no: 9362

Iron girders supplied	10 units @ 1,100	11,000
	VAT @ 20%	2,200
	Total	13,400

(c)   **Identify TWO discrepancies in the invoice received.**

Discrepancy	✓
Date of invoice	
Product type	
Quantity of product	
Unit price	
VAT rate	
Total	

41   NORMAN PRICE & CO

The supplier invoice below has been received.

Henry's Office Supplies	
To: Norman Price & Co	Date: 14 March 20XX
Invoice number: 7208	£
Supply and fit office desks x 2	584.00
VAT @ 20%	116.80
Total	700.80

(a)   **Identify the daybook in which the invoice will be entered.**

Daybook	✓
Sales daybook	
Purchases daybook	
Cashbook	
Purchase returns daybook	
Sales returns daybook	
Discounts allowed daybook	

(b)   Complete the daybook by:

- Making FOUR entries to record the invoice

- Totalling the net, VAT and total columns.

Date 20XX	Supplier	Invoice number	Net £	VAT £	Total £
8 Mar	Norris Ltd	3897	1,010.00	202.00	1,212.00
10 Mar	Sam Jones	0187	878.40	175.68	1,054.08
11 Mar	James & Sarah Ltd	402929	463.80	92.76	556.56
11 Mar	Trevor Dylis Ltd	73910	1,329.10	265.82	1,594.92
14 Mar	Henry's Office Supplies				
		Totals			

The following credit note and invoice relates to a prompt payment discount taken by Norman Price & Co.

George's Printer Repairs	
To: Norman Price & Co	Date: 28 March 20XX
Invoice number: 549	£
Printer repair work	675.00
VAT @ 20%	135.00
Total	810.00
Payment terms: 30 days from end of month of invoice. 2% discount if payment received within 14 days.	

George's Printer Repairs	
To: Norman Price & Co	Date: 4 Apr 20XX
Credit note number: CN45	£
To adjust invoice 548 for prompt payment discount	13.50
VAT @ 20%	2.60
Total	16.10

(c) Identify TWO discrepancies between the invoice and the credit note.

Discrepancy	✓
Prompt payment discount value	
VAT	
Invoice number	
Total	

42 FREDDIE LTD

Purchase invoices have been received and partially entered in the purchases daybook of Freddie Ltd, as shown below.

Novot & Co

5 Pheasant Way, Essex, ES9 8BN

VAT Registration No. 453 098 541

Invoice No. 2176

Freddie Ltd

9 Banbury Street

Sheffield

31 July 20XX

10 boxes of product code 14212 @ £400 each	£4,000
VAT	£800
Total	£4,800

Payment terms 30 days

Purchases daybook

Date 20XX	Details	Invoice number	Total £	VAT £	Net £	Product 14211 £	Product 14212 £
31 July	Box Ltd	2177			800	800	
31 July	Shrew Ltd	2175		2,400		12,000	
31 July	Novot & Co	2176					
	Totals						

(a) Complete the first two entries in the purchases daybook by inserting the appropriate figures for each invoice.

(b) Complete the final entry in the purchases daybook by inserting the appropriate figures from the invoice above and complete the daybook totals.

43   ALPHA LTD

Shown below is a statement of account received from a credit supplier, and the supplier's account as shown in the payables ledger of Alpha Ltd.

ABG Ltd

14 Hassle Street, Durham, DH9 7RQ

To: Alpha Ltd

121 Baker St

Newcastle, NE1 7DJ

STATEMENT OF ACCOUNT

Date 20XX	Invoice number	Details	Invoice amount £	Cheque amount £	Balance £
1 May	468	Goods	7,600		7,600
1 June		Cheque		2,500	5,100
5 June	472	Goods	4,200		9,300
12 June	478	Goods	500		9,800
22 June	486	Goods	1,680		11,480
30 June		Cheque		2,000	9,480

ABG Ltd

Date 20XX	Details	Amount £	Date 20XX	Details	Amount £
4 June	Bank	2,500	3 May	Purchases	7,600
28 June	Bank	2,000	8 June	Purchases	4,200
28 July	Purchase return	900	15 June	Purchases	500

(a)   Which item is missing from the statement of account from ABG Ltd?

[   ]

Picklist: Cheque for £2,500, invoice 468, Invoice 472, Purchase return £900, Invoice 486, Cheque for £2,000

(b)   Which item is missing from the supplier account in Alpha Ltd's payables ledger?

[   ]

Picklist: Invoice 468, Invoice 472, Invoice 478, Invoice 486, Purchase return £900, Cheque for £2,500

(c)   Once the omitted items have been recorded, what is the agreed balance outstanding between Alpha Ltd and ABG Ltd?

[   ]

44 MAXIMUS LTD

Alpha Ltd sends out cheques to suppliers on the last day of the month following the month of invoice. Below is an extract from the purchases (payables) ledger of Alpha Ltd.

Maximus Ltd

Date 20XX	Details	Amount £	Date 20XX	Details	Amount £
15 July	Purchases returns credit note 252	964	1 July	Balance b/f	5,980
21 July	Purchase return credit note 258	1,218	12 July	Purchases Invoice 864	6,386
31 July	Bank	5,980			

(a) Complete the remittance advice note below.

<table>
<tr><td colspan="3" align="center">

Alpha Ltd

121 Baker St

Newcastle, NE1 7DJ

REMITTANCE ADVICE
</td></tr>
<tr><td colspan="3">**To:** Maximus Ltd 20XX   **Date:** 31 Aug

Please find attached our cheque in payment of the following amounts.</td></tr>
<tr><td align="center">**Invoice number**</td><td align="center">**Credit note number**</td><td align="center">**Amount £**</td></tr>
<tr><td></td><td></td><td></td></tr>
<tr><td></td><td></td><td></td></tr>
<tr><td></td><td></td><td></td></tr>
<tr><td></td><td></td><td></td></tr>
<tr><td></td><td></td><td></td></tr>
<tr><td colspan="2" align="right">**Total amount paid**</td><td></td></tr>
</table>

(b) Are these two statements true or false?

A remittance note is for our records only   T / F

A remittance note is sent to a supplier to advise them of the amount being paid   T / F

45   HOLLY LTD

The account shown below is in the payables ledger of AD Wholesale. A cheque for £4,770 has now been paid to this supplier.

Holly Ltd

Date 20XX	Details	Amount £	Date 20XX	Details	Amount £
			5 Jan	Balance b/f	1,500
15 Jan	Purchase return 251	540	19 Jan	Purchase invoice 3658	2,360
31 Jan	Purchase return 286	360	27 Jan	Purchase invoice 2987	1,450

(a)   Which item has been not been included in the payment, causing it to be overstated?

Picklist: Balance b/f, Purchase invoice 3658, Bank, Purchase returns 286, Purchase invoice 2987

An invoice has been received from Rickman Repairs for £860 plus VAT of £172. A prompt payment discount of 10% will be offered for payment within 30 days.

(b)   What is the amount we should pay, if we meet the 30 days requirement?

£

(c)   How much VAT is payable if the payment is NOT made in 30 days?

£

(d)   What is the amount we should pay if payment is NOT made within 30 days?

£

46   EP MANUFACTURERS

Shown below is a statement of account received from a credit supplier, and the supplier's account as shown in the payables ledger of EP Manufacturers.

KLP Ltd

19 Mussell Street, Newcastle, NE4 8JH

To: EP Manufacturers

19 Edmund St

Newcastle, NE6 5DJ

STATEMENT OF ACCOUNT

Date 20XX	Invoice number	Details	Invoice amount £	Cheque amount £	Balance £
1 Jan	468	Goods	5,200		5,200
3 Jan	458	Goods	3,600		8,800
8 Jan		Cheque		1,400	7,400
19 Jan	478	Goods	800		8,200
21 Jan		Cheque		6,500	1,700
28 Jan	488	Goods	4,350		6,050

KLP Ltd

Date 20XX	Details	Amount £	Date 20XX	Details	Amount £
8 Jan	Bank	1,400	1 Jan	Purchases	5,200
21 Jan	Bank	6,500	3 Jan	Purchases	3,600
31 Jan	Bank	1,200	19 Jan	Purchases	800

(a)   **Which item is missing from the statement of account from KLP Ltd?**

Picklist: Cheque for £1,200, invoice 468, Invoice 478, Cheque for £6,500, Invoice 488, Cheque for £1,400

(b)   **Which item is missing from the supplier account in EP Manufacturers' payables ledger?**

Picklist: Invoice 468, Invoice 472, Invoice 478, Invoice 488, Purchase return £900, Cheque for £2,500

(c)   **Once the omitted items have been recorded, what is the agreed balance outstanding between EP Manufacturers and KLP Ltd?**

£

47   STANNY LTD

Ringo's Rings sends out cheques to suppliers on the last day of the month following the month of invoice. Below is an extract from the payables ledger of Ringo's Rings.

Stanny Ltd

Date 20XX	Details	Amount £	Date 20XX	Details	Amount £
13 Feb	Purchases returns credit note 198	650	1 Feb	Balance b/f	4,650
19 Feb	Purchase return credit note 154	1,250	10 Feb	Purchases Invoice 694	2,300
28 Feb	Bank	4,650	11 Feb	Purchase invoice 658	3,640

(a)   Complete the remittance advice note below.

Ringo Rings

37 Parker Lane

Stoke SK1 0KE

REMITTANCE ADVICE

To: Stanny Ltd   **Date:** 31 Mar 20XX

Please find attached our cheque in payment of the following amounts.

Invoice number	Credit note number	Amount £
	Total amount paid	

(b)   Are these two statements true or false?

A remittance note is for our and the supplier's records   T / F

A remittance note is sent by a supplier confirming amounts received from them   T / F

48   TOYWORLD

Shown below is a statement of account received from a credit supplier, and the supplier's account as shown in the payables ledger of Hickory House

Toyworld
18 Landview Road
Skipton
BD27 4TU

To: Hickory House
22 Nursery Road
Keighley, BD22 7BD

STATEMENT OF ACCOUNT

Date 20XX	Invoice number	Details	Invoice amount £	Cheque amount £	Balance £
1 Jan	207	Goods	2,500		2,500
8 April	310	Goods	900		3,400
9 June		Cheque		3,400	0
17 Aug	504	Goods	500		500
18 Aug	505	Goods	4,000		4,500

Toyworld

Date 20XX	Details	Amount £	Date 20XX	Details	Amount £
9 June	Bank	3,400	1 Jan	Purchases	2,500
25 June	Bank	500	8 April	Purchases	900
			17 Aug	Purchases	500

(a)   **Which item is missing from the statement of account from Toyworld?**

[   ]

Picklist: Invoice 207, Invoice 310, Invoice 504, Invoice 505, Cheque for £3,400, Cheque for £500

(b)   **Which item is missing from the supplier account in Hickory Houses' payables ledger?**

[   ]

Picklist: Invoice 207, Invoice 310, Invoice 504, Invoice 505, Cheque for £3,400, Cheque for £500

(c)   **Assuming any differences between the statement of account from Toyworld and the supplier account in Hickory Houses' payables ledger are simply due to omission errors, what is the amount owing to Toyworld?**

£ [   ]

49   HENRY HOUSE

Henry House sends out cheques to suppliers on the last day of the month following the month of invoice. Below is an extract from the payables ledger of Henry House.

Abbies Party Ltd

Date 20XX	Details	Amount £	Date 20XX	Details	Amount £
17 July	Purchases returns credit note 27	82	15 July	Purchases Invoice 242	220
			10 Aug	Purchases Invoice 764	44

(a)   Complete the remittance advice note below.

<table>
<tr><td colspan="3" align="center">

Henry House

22 Nursery Road

Keighley, BD22 7BD

REMITTANCE ADVICE

To: Abbies Party

Date: 31 August 20XX

Please find attached our cheque in payment of the following amounts.

</td></tr>
</table>

Invoice number	Credit note number	Amount £
	Total amount paid	

(b)   Which of the following statements is true?

A   The remittance advice note will be sent to the Inventory Dept to advise them inventory has been paid for

B   The remittance advice note will be sent to the customer to advise them of the amount being paid

C   The remittance advice note will be sent to Henry House's bank to confirm payment is to be made

D   The remittance advice note will be sent to the supplier to advise them of the amount being paid

50   GREY GARAGES

Grey Garages makes payments to suppliers by BACS on the 25th of every month and includes all items that have been outstanding for more than 10 days.

Below is a pre-printed remittance advice slip taken from a statement of account received from a supplier, Mulberry Motors, showing all items outstanding.

Complete the remittance advice ready for the next payment to Mulberry Motors.

Remittance advice			
To: Mulberry Motors			
From: Grey Garages			
Payment method:		**Date of payment:**	

Items outstanding			**Tick if included in payment**
Date 20XX	**Details**	**Amount** £	
23-Jun	Invoice 213	740	
06-Jul	Credit note 14	120	
13-Jul	Invoice 216	620	
19-Jul	Invoice 257	870	
		Total amount paid	£

51   ERRICO

The two invoices below were received on 5 June from credit suppliers who offer prompt payment discounts.

Invoices:

Giacomo

VAT registration 446 1552 01

Invoice number 1923

To: Errico	4 June 20XX
	£
4 product code 45 @ £14.50 each	58.00
VAT @ 20%	11.60
	————
Total	69.60

Terms: 3% prompt payment discount if payment is received within 7 days of the invoice date.

Gaetani

VAT registration 446 4742 01

Invoice number 4578

To: Errico	4 June 20XX
	£
3 product code 42a @ £11.50 each	34.50
VAT @ 20%	6.90
	————
Total	41.40

Terms: 5% prompt payment discount if payment is received within 5 days of the invoice date.

Calculate the amount to be paid to each supplier if the prompt payment discount is taken and show the date by which the supplier should receive the payment.

Supplier	£	Date by which the payment should be received by the supplier
Giacomo		
Gaetani		

52 LEWIN & CO

The two invoices below were received on 20 October from credit suppliers of Lewin & Co who offer prompt payment discounts.

Invoices:

Bridge Brothers

VAT registration 446 4752 01

Invoice number 193

To: Lewin & Co   19 October 20XX

	£
5 product code 895 @ £18.75 each	93.75
VAT @ 20%	18.75
	———
Total	112.50

Terms: 2% prompt payment discount if payment is received within 4 days of the invoice date.

Mitchells

VAT registration 446 4742 01

Invoice number 578

To: Lewin & Co   19 October 20XX

	£
9 product code 756 @ £13.25 each	119.25
VAT @ 20%	23.85
	———
Total	143.10

Terms: 10% prompt payment discount if payment is received within 5 days of the invoice date.

(a)   Calculate the amount to be paid to each supplier if the prompt payment discount is taken and show the date by which the supplier should receive the payment.

Supplier	£	Date by which the payment should be received by the supplier
Bridge Brothers		
Mitchells		

It is the policy of Lewin & Co to check each supplier statement as they arrive to ensure that they agree to the individual accounts within the payables ledger. Provided below is the statement of account from Xcess Stock and their account in the payables ledger.

Lewin & Co's policy is to only pay for items from the supplier statement which appear in their account in the payables ledger.

(b) **Place a tick next to the 3 items in the supplier statement which will not be included within the payment.**

Date 20XX	Details	Amount £	Date 20XX	Details	Amount £
21 Dec	Credit note 101	940	12 Dec	Invoice 1001	1,700
			21 Dec	Invoice 1004	2,350
31 Dec	Balance c/d	3,580	27 Dec	Invoice 1010	470
		4,520			4,520
			20XY 1 Jan	Balance b/d	3,580

Xcess Stock Unit 7 Windy Industrial Estate Irvine, KA6 8HU **To:** Lewin & Co **Date:** 31 Dec 20XX			**Not to be paid** ✓
Date 20XX	**Details**	**Transaction amount £**	
12 Dec	Invoice 1001	1,700	
13 Dec	Invoice 1003	1,500	
21 Dec	Invoice 1004	2,350	
21 Dec	Credit note 101	940	
22 Dec	Invoice 1005	450	
27 Dec	Invoice 1010	470	
28 Dec	Credit note 102	50	

(c) **What will be the amount paid to Xcess Stock by Lewin & Co?**

£

(d)   One of the accounts within the payables ledger of Lewin & Co is for the credit supplier Minto Madness. A credit note for a prompt payment discount of £20 plus VAT has been received from Minto Madness. Before processing the credit note, the balance on the account of Minto Madness is £1,540.

What is the amount remaining on the account taking into consideration the credit note?

£

53   ASHBOURNE LTD

It is company policy at Ashbourne Ltd to only take advantage of prompt payment discount if the discount percentage is at least 5%. Below is a report from the digital bookkeeping system dated today, 13 January.

Supplier account code	Supplier name	Payment terms
K17	Kennack & Co	30 days
B07	Butterworth & Sons	30 days (4% discount for payments within 10 days)
J04	Jermyn Ltd	30 days (5% discount for payments within 7 days)

(a)   **Identify the amount to be paid and the date by which the supplier should receive payment, for each of the invoices below:**

Supplier name	Invoice amount £	Invoice date 20XX	Amount to be paid £	Date by which supplier should receive payment
Kennack & Co	756.90	9 Jan		
Butterworth & Sons	1,317.83	11 Jan		
Jermyn Ltd	847.60	10 Jan		

Below is a statement of account from a supplier, as well as a supplier report from the digital bookkeeping system.

Farfield Ltd Statement of Account			Supplier report		
To: Ashbourne Ltd		30 June 20XX	Farfield Ltd	Supplier code F009	
Date 20XX	Transactions	£	Date 20XX	Details	£
1 June	Opening balance	639	1 June	Opening balance	639
4 June	Invoice 287	1,204	4 June	Invoice 287	1,204
8 June	Invoice 294	897	8 June	Invoice 294	897
11 June	Invoice 304	3,453	11 June	Invoice 304	3,453
12 June	Invoice 307	257	12 June	Invoice 307	257
18 June	Credit note 045	564	12 June	Invoice 307	257
26 June	Invoice 342	1,865	18 June	Credit note 045	564
			26 June	Invoice 342	1,865
			30 June	CHQ 3672	5,296

(b) Identify which **THREE** transactions shown on the supplier statement of account have already been paid.

Transactions	✓
Opening balance	
Invoice 287	
Invoice 294	
Invoice 304	
Invoice 307	
Invoice 307	
Credit note 045	
Invoice 342	

(c)   Identify the type of error shown on the supplier report on the 12 June.

Type of error	✓
Underpayment	
Overpayment	
Missing transactions	
Duplicate transaction	
Timing difference	

54   FARFIELD LTD

It is company policy at Farfield Ltd to always take advantage of prompt payment discount offered. Below is a report from the digital bookkeeping system dated today, 28 August.

Supplier account code	Supplier name	Payment terms
A09	Archer Joinery	Net monthly
S06	Sankey Electrical	2.5% discount for payments within 14 days
P05	Pannal Construction	3% discount for payments within 10 days

(a)   Identify the amount to be paid and the date by which the supplier should receive payment, for each of the invoices below:

Supplier name	Invoice amount £	Invoice date 20XX	Amount to be paid £	Date by which supplier should receive payment
Archer Joinery	1,340.00	25 Aug		
Sankey Electrical	4,372.80	26 Aug		
Pannal Construction	3,720.00	26 Aug		

Below is a statement of account from a supplier, as well as a supplier report from the digital bookkeeping system.

Kelham Builders Statement of Account			Supplier report		
To: Farfield Ltd		**31 Oct 20XX**	**Kelham Builders**	**Supplier code K06**	
Date 20XX	**Transactions**	**£**	**Date 20XX**	**Details**	**£**
1 Oct	Opening balance	2,056	1 Oct	Opening balance	1,160
2 Oct	CHQ 0786	896	7 Oct	Invoice 308	945
7 Oct	Invoice 308	945	10 Oct	Invoice 314	1,342
10 Oct	Invoice 314	1,342	14 Oct	Credit note 048	897
14 Oct	Credit note 048	897	22 Oct	Invoice 326	2,085
22 Oct	Invoice 326	2,085	26 Oct	Invoice 338	451
26 Oct	Invoice 338	451	29 Oct	CHQ 0831	1,605
30 Oct	Invoice 343	846	30 Oct	Invoice 343	846

(b)   Identify which THREE transactions shown on the supplier statement of account have already been paid.

Transactions	✓
Opening balance	
Invoice 308	
Invoice 314	
Credit note 048	
Invoice 326	
Invoice 338	
Invoice 343	

(c) **Identify the reason for the discrepancy between the opening balance on the supplier statement and the supplier report.**

Type of error	✓
Underpayment	
Timing difference	
Overpayment	
Missing transactions	
Duplicate transaction	

PROCESS RECEIPTS AND PAYMENTS

55 ABC LTD

There are five payments to be entered in ABC Ltd's cash book.

Receipts

Received cash with thanks for goods bought. From ABC Ltd, a customer without a credit account. Net £180 VAT £36 Total £216 S. Lampard	Received cash with thanks for goods bought. From ABC Ltd, a customer without a credit account. Net £220 VAT £44 Total £264 S Bobbins	Received cash with thanks for goods bought. ABC Ltd, a customer without a credit account. Net £530 (No VAT) Penny Rhodes

Cheque book counterfoils

Henley's Ltd (Payables ledger account HEN002) £4,925 000372	Epic Equipment Maintenance (We have no credit account with this supplier) £480 incl VAT 000373

(a)   **Enter the details from the three receipts and two cheque book stubs into the credit side of the cash book shown below and total each column.**

Cash book – Credit side

Details	Cash	Bank	VAT	Payables	Cash purchases	Repairs and renewals
Balance b/f						
S. Lampard						
S. Bobbins						
Penny Rhodes						
Henley's Ltd						
Epic Equipment Maintenance						
Total						

There are two cheques from credit customers to be entered in ABC Ltd's cash book:

D. Davies   £851

E. Denholm   £450

(b)   **Enter the above details into the debit side of the cash book and total each column.**

Cash book – Debit side

Details	Cash	Bank	Receivables
Balance b/f	1,550	7,425	
D Davies			
E Denholm			
Total			

(c)   **Using your answers to (a) and (b) above calculate the cash balance.**

£

(d)   **Using your answers to (a) and (b) above calculate the bank balance.**

£

(e)   **Will the bank balance calculated in (d) above be a debit or credit balance?**

Debit/Credit

56   BEDS

There are five payments to be entered in Beds' cash book.

Receipts

Received cash with thanks for goods bought.	Received cash with thanks for goods bought.	Received cash with thanks for goods bought.
From Beds, a customer without a credit account.	From Beds, a customer without a credit account.	From Beds, a customer without a credit account.
Net £590 VAT £118 Total £708	Net £190 VAT £38 Total £228	Net £230 (No VAT)
A. Blighty Ltd	R Bromby	Roxy Bland

Cheque book counterfoils

Burgess Ltd (Payables ledger account BUR003) £2,400 000101	Fast Equipment Repairs (We have no credit account with this supplier) £96 including VAT 000102

(a)   **Enter the details from the three receipts and two cheque book stubs into the credit side of the cash book shown below and total each column.**

Cash book – Credit side

Details	Cash	Bank	VAT	Payables	Cash purchases	Repairs and renewals
Balance b/f						
A. Blighty Ltd						
R Bromby						
Roxy Bland						
Burgess Ltd						
Fast Equipment Repairs						
Total						

There are two cheques from credit customers to be entered in Beds' cash book:

A. Barnett   £698

H. Connelly   £250

(b)   Enter the above details into the debit side of the cash book and total each column.

Cash book – Debit side

Details	Cash	Bank	Receivables
Balance b/f	1,175	3,825	
A Barnett			
H Connelly			
Total			

(c)   Using your answers to (a) and (b) above calculate the cash balance.

£

(d)   Using your answers to (a) and (b) above calculate the bank balance.

£

(e)   Will the bank balance calculated in (d) above be a debit or credit balance?

Debit/Credit

57   JO'S

There are five payments to be entered into Jo's cash book.

Receipts

Received cash with thanks for good bought.	Received cash with thanks for good bought.	Received cash with thanks for good bought.
From Jo's, a customer without a credit account.	From Jo's, a customer without a credit account.	From Jo's, a customer without a credit account.
Net £40	Net £80	Net £455
VAT £8	VAT £16	(no VAT)
Total £48	Total £96	
T. Hunkin Ltd	Victoria Green	B. Head Ltd

Cheque book counterfoils

Smiths Ltd	Arrow Valley Stationers
(Payables ledger account SMI527)	(We have no credit account with this supplier)
£4,250	£120 (including VAT)
001456	001457

(a)   Enter the details from the three receipts and two cheque book stubs into the credit side of the cash book shown below and total each column.

Cash book – credit side

Details	Cash	Bank	VAT	Payables	Cash purchases	Stationery expenses
Bal b/f		19,546				
T. Hunkin Ltd						
Victoria Green						
B. Head Ltd						
Smiths Ltd						
Arrow Valley Stationers						
Total						

There are two cheques from credit customers to be entered into Jo's cash book:

J Drummond   £623

N Atkinson   £425

(b)   Enter the above details into the debit side of the cash book below and total each column.

Cash book – debit side

Details	Cash	Bank	Receivables
Balance b/f	986		
J Drummond			
N Atkinson			
Total			

(c)   Using your answers to (a) and (b) above calculate the cash balance.

£ _____

(d)   Using your answers to (a) and (b) above calculate the bank balance.

£ _____

(e)   Will the bank balance calculated in (d) above be a debit or a credit balance?

Debit/Credit

58   CARTER

There are five payments to be entered in Carter's cash book.

Receipts

Received cash with thanks for goods bought. From Carter's, a customer without a credit account. Net £800 VAT £160 Total £960 J Pumpkin	Received cash with thanks for goods bought. From Carter's, a customer without a credit account. Net £200 VAT £40 Total £240 B Row

Cheque book counterfoils

Lemon Ltd (Payables ledger account LEM002) £100 000123	**Remo Motor** (no credit account) £240 including VAT 000124	**Fencer** (Payables ledger account FEN001) £600 000125

(a)   Enter the details from the two receipts and three cheque book stubs into the credit side of the cash book shown below and total each column.

Cash book – Credit side

Details	Cash	Bank	VAT	Payables	Cash purchases	Motor expenses
Balance b/f		11,450				
J Pumpkin						
B Row						
Lemon Ltd						
Remo Motor						
Fencer						
Total						

There are two cheques from credit customers to be entered in Carter's cash book:

Jeff Jolly £127

Dolly Darton £310

(b) **Enter the above details into the debit side of the cash book and total each column.**

Cash book – Debit side

Details	Cash	Bank	Receivables
Balance b/f	1,850		
Jeff Jolly			
Dolly Darton			
Total			

(c) **Using your answers to (a) and (b) above, calculate the cash balance.**

£

(d) **Using your answers to (a) and (b) above, calculate the bank balance.**

£

(e) **Will the bank balance calculated in (d) above be a debit or credit balance?**

Debit/Credit

59   MANGROVE

Three amounts have been paid as shown in the payments listing below.

Date 20XX	Supplier account code	Supplier name	Cash £	Cheque £
25 May	–	K Quick – cash supplier	£279.00 (exc VAT)	
26 May	WHIL07	Whiles Ltd – credit supplier		£1,374.00 (inc. VAT)
27 May	SASH12	Sasha and Co – cash supplier		£418.80 (inc VAT)

Complete the credit side of the cash book by making the necessary entries.

Date 20XX	Details	Cash £	Bank £	VAT £	Cash purchases	Payables £
25 May	K Quick					
26 May	Whiles Ltd					
27 May	Sasha and Co					

60 SWAMP

Two amounts have been received as shown in the receipts listing below.

Date 20XX	Customer account code	Customer name	Cash £	Cheque £
23 Aug	BENN12	Bennett Ltd – credit customer		£2,924.40 (inc. VAT)
25 Aug	–	J Smith – cash customer	£488.80 (exc. VAT)	

(a) **Complete the debit side of the cash book by making the necessary entries.**

Date 20XX	Details	Cash £	Bank £	VAT £	Cash sales	Receiv-ables
23 Aug	Bal b/f	1,089.70	8,539.43			
23 Aug	Bennett Ltd					
25 Aug	J Smith					

The credit side of the cash book shows that the total cash payments were £813.48.

(b) **Calculate the cash balance.**

£	

61 QUEEN VIC

Part way through the month the petty cash account had a balance of £145.00. The cash in the petty cash box was checked and the following notes and coins were there.

Notes and coins	£
4 × £20 notes	80.00
1 × £10 notes	10.00
2 × £5 notes	10.00
12 × £1 coins	12.00
40 × 50p coins	20.00
45 × 20p coins	9.00

(a) **Reconcile the cash amount in the petty cash box with the balance on the petty cash account.**

Amount in petty cash box	£
Balance on petty cash account	£
Difference	£

At the end of the month the cash in the petty cash box was £27.25

(b) **Complete the petty cash reimbursement document below to restore the imprest amount of £150.**

Petty cash reimbursement	
Date: 31.07.20XX	
Amount required to restore the cash in the petty cash box.	£

62 THE ARCHES

This is a summary of petty cash payments made by The Arches.

Mick's Motors paid	£20.00 (no VAT)
Stamps paid	£19.00 (no VAT)
Office Essentials paid	£22.00 plus VAT

(a) **Enter the above transactions, in the order in which they are shown, in the petty cash book below.**

(b) **Total the petty cash book and show the balance carried down.**

Petty cash book

Debit side		Credit side					
Details	Amount £	Details	Amount £	VAT £	Postage £	Travel £	Stationery £
Balance b/f	200.00					20.00	

Picklist: Amount, Balance b/d, Balance c/d, Details, Postage, Stamps, Stationery, Office Essentials, Mick's Motors, VAT, Travel

63   RAINBOW

This is a summary of petty cash payments made by Rainbow.

Colin's Cabs paid	£28.00 (no VAT)
Post Office paid	£18.00 (no VAT)
ABC Stationery paid	£32.00 plus VAT

(a)   **Enter the above transactions, in the order in which they are shown, in the petty cash book below.**

(b)   **Total the petty cash book and show the balance carried down.**

Petty cash book

Debit side		Credit side					
Details	Amount £	Details	Amount £	VAT £	Postage £	Travel £	Stationery £
Balance b/f	100.00						

Picklist: Amount, Balance b/d, Balance c/d, Details, Postage, Post Office, Stationery, ABC Stationery, Colin's Cabs, VAT, Travel

64   SOOTY & SWEEP

Part way through the month the petty cash account had a balance of £135.00. The cash in the petty cash box was checked and the following notes and coins were there.

Notes and coins	£
2 × £20 notes	40.00
6 × £10 notes	60.00
15 × £1 coins	15.00
18 × 50p coins	9.00
12 × 20p coins	2.40
10 × 10p coins	1.00

(a)   **Reconcile the cash amount in the petty cash box with the balance on the petty cash account.**

Amount in petty cash box	£
Balance on petty cash account	£
Difference	£

At the end of the month the cash in the petty cash box was £5.00

(b) **Complete the petty cash reimbursement document below to restore the imprest amount of £250.**

Petty cash reimbursement	
Date: 31.07.20XX	
Amount required to restore the cash in the petty cash box.	£

65 JAWS DENTISTRY

This is a summary of petty cash payments made by Jaws Dentistry.

Ace Taxis paid	£26.00 (no VAT)
Kate's Couriers	£27.00 (no VAT)
Smiths Stationery	£38.00 plus VAT

(a) **Enter the above transactions, in the order in which they are shown, in the petty cash book below.**

(b) **Total the petty cash book and show the balance carried down.**

Petty cash book

Debit side		Credit side					
Details	Amount £	Details	Amount £	VAT £	Postage £	Travel £	Stationery £
Balance b/f	225.00						

Picklist: Amount, Balance b/d, Balance c/d, Details, Postage, Kate's Couriers, Smiths Stationery, Ace Taxis, Travel, VAT.

66 TOM'S TILES

Part way through the month the petty cash account had a balance of £165.52. The cash in the petty cash box was checked and the following notes and coins were there.

Notes and coins	£
4 × £20 notes	80.00
4 × £10 notes	40.00
3 × £5 notes	15.00
18 × £1 coins	18.00
7 × 50p coins	3.50
18 × 20p coins	3.60
19 × 10p coins	1.90
6 × 2p coins	0.12

(a) **Reconcile the cash amount in the petty cash box with the balance on the petty cash account.**

	£
Amount in petty cash box	£
Balance on petty cash account	£
Difference	£

At the end of the month the cash in the petty cash box was £25.88.

(b) **Complete the petty cash reimbursement document below to restore the imprest amount of £250.00.**

Petty cash reimbursement	
Date: 30.04.20XX	
Amount required to restore the cash in the petty cash box.	£

67 ROCKY RILEY

This is a summary of petty cash payments made by Rocky Riley.

Kath's Kars paid	£32.00 (no VAT)
Stamps paid	£25.00 (no VAT)
Pauline's Pens paid	£20.00 plus VAT

(a) Enter the above transactions, in the order in which they are shown, in the petty cash book below.

(b) Total the petty cash book and show the balance carried down.

Petty cash book

Debit side		Credit side					
Details	Amount £	Details	Amount £	VAT £	Postage £	Travel £	Stationery £
Balance b/f	175.00						

Picklist: Amount, Balance b/d, Balance c/d, Details, Postage, Stamps, Stationery, Pauline's Pens, Kath's Kars, Travel, VAT

68 MHAIRI MOTORS

Part way through the month the petty cash account had a balance of £110.00. The cash in the petty cash box was checked and the following notes and coins were there.

Notes and coins	£
5 × £10 notes	50.00
5 × £5 notes	25.00
4 × £1 coins	4.00
11 × 50p coins	5.50
75 × 20p coins	15.00
3 × 10p coins	0.30

(a) Reconcile the cash amount in the petty cash box with the balance on the petty cash account.

Amount in petty cash box	£
Balance on petty cash account	£
Difference	£

At the end of the month the cash in the petty cash box was £8.50

(b) **Complete the petty cash reimbursement document below to restore the imprest amount of £200.**

Petty cash reimbursement	
Date: 31.07.20XX	
Amount required to restore the cash in the petty cash box.	£

69 DAINTY DESIGNS

Dainty Designs keeps an analytical petty cash book.

On 31 March there was one final petty cash payment to be recorded in the petty cash book.

An amount of £31.20 including VAT had been paid for fuel expenses.

(a) **Calculate the VAT and net amounts to be recorded in the petty cash book.**

VAT £	Net £

Before the petty cash payment in (a) was recorded, amounts totalling £65.66 had been entered into the fuel expenses analysis column of the petty cash book.

(b) **Calculate the total of the fuel expenses analysis column after the petty cash payment in (a) has been recorded.**

£

After all March petty cash payments had been made, an amount of £42.30 was left in the petty cash float.

This agreed with the total of all payments now recorded in the petty cash book of £233.90. On 31 March the petty cash float was topped up to £280.

(c) **What will be the entry in the petty cash book to record this transaction?**

Details	Amount £	Debit ✓	Credit ✓

Picklist: Balance b/d, Balance c/d, Cash from bank

(d) **What will be the entry in the petty cash book to record the closing balance on 31 March?**

Details	Amount £	Debit ✓	Credit ✓

Picklist: Balance b/d, Balance c/d, Cash from bank

On 2 April the following petty cash vouchers are ready to be recorded:

Petty cash voucher 222

2 April 20X7

Diesel

£27.00 plus VAT

Petty cash voucher 223

2 April 20X7

Lever arch files

£12.00 including VAT

(e) **What will be the total, VAT and net amounts to be entered into the petty cash book?**

Petty cash voucher	Total £	VAT £	Net £
222			
223			

70 JACKSON MOTORING

Jackson Motoring keeps an analytical petty cash book.

On 31 October there was one final petty cash payment to be recorded in the petty cash book.

An amount of £21.60 including VAT had been paid for stationery expenses.

(a) **Calculate the VAT and net amounts to be recorded in the petty cash book.**

VAT £	Net £

Before the petty cash payment in (a) was recorded, amounts totalling £15.50 had been entered into the stationery expenses analysis column of the petty cash book.

(b) **Calculate the total of the stationery expenses analysis column after the petty cash payment in (a) has been recorded.**

£

After all October petty cash payments had been made, an amount of £31.55 was left in the petty cash float.

This agreed with the total of all payments now recorded in the petty cash book of £152.40. On 31 October the petty cash float was topped up to £215.

(c)   **What will be the entry in the petty cash book to record this transaction?**

Details	Amount £	Debit ✓	Credit ✓

Picklist: Balance b/d, Balance c/d, Cash from bank

(d)   **What will be the entry in the petty cash book to record the closing balance on 31 October?**

Details	Amount £	Debit ✓	Credit ✓

Picklist: Balance b/d, Balance c/d, Cash from bank

On 2 November the following petty cash vouchers are ready to be recorded:

Petty cash voucher 120

2 November 20X7

FST Taxis

£20 (no VAT)

Petty cash voucher 121

2 November 20X7

Pens

£19.20 including VAT

(e)   **What will be the total, VAT and net amounts to be entered into the petty cash book?**

Petty cash voucher	Total £	VAT £	Net £
120			
121			

71 WHILES LTD

Whiles Ltd uses an imprest system for petty cash alongside an analysed petty cash book. At the end of October, the cash remaining in the petty cash float was £47.83. The total value of the petty cash vouchers was £302.17.

On 1 November the petty cash imprest amount was replenished.

(a) **Identify the correct entry required in the petty cash book to record this transaction.**

Details	Amount £	Debit ✓	Credit ✓
See below			

Details	✓
Balance brought down	
Bank	
Sales	
Cash	

When reconciling the petty cash book and vouchers for November, the following was discovered:

- The sum of the petty cash vouchers is £196.22

- The total amount of petty cash expenditure recorded in the petty cash book is £216.22

(b) **Which TWO of the following could explain this discrepancy?**

	✓
A missing petty cash voucher for £16.67 excluding VAT	
Cash of £20 has been stolen from petty cash	
A petty cash voucher for £20 has yet to be recorded in the petty cash book	
A petty cash transaction of £64.20 was incorrectly recorded in the petty cash book as £84.20	

Before recording the final petty cash transaction in December, cleaning expenses of £48.00 including VAT had been recorded in the petty cash book. The final petty cash payment to be recorded was a payment of £24.00 excluding VAT for cleaning expenses

(c) **Calculate the balance in the cleaning expenses analysis column after this final transaction has been recorded.**

£	

72 BAKER LTD

Baker Ltd uses an imprest system for petty cash alongside an analysed petty cash book. On 30 November there were 2 petty cash transactions left to record as follows:

A payment for window cleaning of £28.50 (including VAT)

A payment for A4 ring binders for £36.00 (excluding VAT)

Complete the petty cash book by making the necessary entries to record these transactions.

Date 20XX	Details	Cash £	VAT £	Cleaning £	Travel £	Food/drink £	Stationery £
30 Nov	Bal b/f	89.40	14.90	14.50	36.00	–	12.00
30 Nov	Window cleaning						
30 Nov	A4 binders						

73 BUTCHER LTD

A new transaction has been arranged, as shown in the note below:

We have entered into a contract today to lease a van for use in the business. The lease will be for a period of 8 months and will cost £250 per month, excluding VAT at 20%. The payments are due on the 5th of each month by standing order, beginning next month.

Please can you set up the recurring accounting entries required?

Thanks,

John Calabassas

17 April 20XX

(a) **Set up the recurring entry in the digital bookkeeping system**

Transaction type	General ledger code	Start date 20XX	End date 20XX	Frequency	Net amount £	VAT code
Bank	Option 1	Option 2	Option 3	Monthly		Option 4

Option 1	✓
7100 – Insurance	
1100 – Van non-current assets	
2000 – Bank	
7400 – Motor lease costs	

Option 2	✓
5 Jun 20XX	
5 May 20XX	
5 Nov 20XX	
5 Dec 20XX	

Option 3	✓
5 Jun 20XX	
5 May 20XX	
5 Nov 20XX	
5 Dec 20XX	

Option 4	✓
V0 – 0%	
V1 – Exempt	
V20 – 20%	
V5 – 5%	

(b) **Identify ONE effect of processing the recurring entry.**

Effect	✓
The standing order will be automatically set up to pay for the lease costs	
Entries will be posted to all relevant general ledger accounts	
Entries will be posted to the receivables ledger and all relevant general ledger accounts	

74 CHANDLER LTD

(a) **Identify which of the following is NOT required in order to set up a recurring entry.**

Information	✓
The number of recurring transactions	
The frequency of the recurring transactions	
The total value of all recurring transactions	
The VAT rate	

A new transaction has been arranged, as shown in the note below:

We have entered into a contract today to provide maintenance services for a new customer, Stepping Stones Ltd. The contract will last for an initial 6 months, and we will receive £480 a month including VAT at 20%. The payments will be made by standing order on the 10th of every month, starting next month.

Please can you set up the recurring entry?

Thanks,

Erica Schwartz

Jan 20XX

(b) **Set up the recurring entry in the digital bookkeeping system.**

Transaction type	General ledger code	Start date 20XX	End date 20XX	Frequency	Net amount £	VAT code
Bank	Option 1	Option 2	Option 3	Monthly		Option 4

Option 1	✓
7560 – Rent expense	
1040 – Office equipment	
2000 – Bank	
4000 – Maintenance services	

Option 2	✓
10 Apr 20XX	
10 May 20XX	
10 Feb 20XX	
10 Jul 20XX	

Option 3	✓
10 Apr 20XX	
10 May 20XX	
10 Feb 20XX	
10 Jul 20XX	

Option 4	✓
V0 – 0%	
V1 – Exempt	
V20 – 20%	
V5 – 5%	

PROCESS TRANSACTIONS INTO LEDGER ACCOUNTS

75   LADY LTD

Given below is the purchases daybook for Lady Ltd.

Date	Invoice No.	Code	Supplier	Total	VAT	Net
1 Dec	03582	PL210	M Brown	300.00	50.00	250.00
5 Dec	03617	PL219	H Madden	183.55	30.59	152.96
7 Dec	03622	PL227	L Singh	132.60	22.10	110.50
10 Dec	03623	PL228	A Stevens	90.00	15.00	75.00
18 Dec	03712	PL301	N Shema	197.08	32.84	164.24
			Totals	903.23	150.53	752.70

You are required to:

*   Post the totals of the purchases daybook to the general ledger accounts given

*   Post the invoices to the payables' accounts in the subsidiary ledger provided.

General ledger

Payables ledger control account

	£			£
			1 Dec Balance b/d	5,103.90

VAT account

	£			£
			1 Dec Balance b/d	526.90

Purchases account

	£		£
1 Dec balance b/d	22,379.52		

Subsidiary ledger

M Brown

	£		£
		1 Dec Balance b/d	68.50

H Madden

	£		£
		1 Dec Balance b/d	286.97

L Singh

	£		£
		1 Dec Balance b/d	125.89

A Stevens

	£		£
		1 Dec Balance b/d	12.36

N Shema

	£		£
		1 Dec Balance b/d	168.70

76 BUTTONS LTD

The following transactions all took place on 31 July and have been entered into the purchases daybook of Buttons Ltd as shown below. No entries have yet been made into the ledger system.

Date 20XX	Details	Invoice number	Total £	VAT £	Net £
31 July	Peak & Co	1720	6,240	1,040	5,200
31 July	Max Ltd	1721	12,720	2,120	10,600
31 July	McIntyre Wholesale	1722	5,760	960	4,800
31 July	Pigmy Ltd	1723	3,744	624	3,120
	Totals		**28,464**	**4,744**	**23,720**

(a) What will be the entries in the payables ledger?

Account name	Amount £	Debit ✓	Credit ✓

Picklist: Peak & Co, Purchases, Receivables ledger control, Purchases returns, McIntyre Wholesale, Sales, Payables ledger control, Max Ltd, Sales returns, VAT, Pigmy Ltd

(b) What will be the entries in the general ledger?

Account name	Amount £	Debit ✓	Credit ✓

Picklist: Payables ledger control, Sales, Receivables ledger control, Purchases, VAT

77 SPARKY LTD

The following credit transactions all took place on 31 July and have been entered into the sales returns daybook of Sparky Ltd as shown below. No entries have yet been made in the ledgers.

Sales returns daybook

Date 20XX	Details	Credit note number	Total £	VAT £	Net £
31 July	Clarkson Ltd	150C	1,680	280	1,400
31 July	Kyle & Co	151C	720	120	600
	Totals		2,400	400	2,000

(a) What will be the entries in the receivables ledger?

Receivables ledger

Account name	Amount £	Debit ✓	Credit ✓

Picklist: Net, Purchases, Payables ledger control, Clarkson Ltd, Purchases returns, Sales, Receivables ledger control, Sales returns, Kyle & Co, Total, VAT

(b) **What will be the entries in the general ledger?**

General ledger

Account name	Amount £	Debit ✓	Credit ✓

Picklist: Kyle & Co, Net, Purchases, Payables ledger control, Purchases returns, Sales, Receivables ledger control, Sales returns, Clarkson Ltd, Total, VAT

78   LOUIS LTD

The following transactions all took place on 31 Jan and have been entered into the sales daybook of Louis Ltd as shown below. No entries have yet been made into the ledger system.

Date 20XX	Details	Invoice number	Total £	VAT £	Net £
31 Jan	Sheep & Co	1400	3,840	640	3,200
31 Jan	Cow Ltd	1401	11,760	1,960	9,800
31 Jan	Chicken & Partners	1402	6,720	1,120	5,600
31 Jan	Pig Ltd	1403	14,496	2,416	12,080
	Totals		36,816	6,136	30,680

(a) **What will be the entries in the receivables ledger?**

Account name	Amount £	Debit ✓	Credit ✓

Picklist: Sheep & Co, Purchases, Receivables ledger control, Cow Ltd, Purchases returns, Sales, Chicken & Partners, Payables ledger control, Sales returns, VAT, Pig Ltd

(b) **What will be the entries in the general ledger?**

Account name	Amount £	Debit ✓	Credit ✓

Picklist: Payables ledger control, Sales, Receivables ledger control, Purchases, VAT

79 THOMAS & TILLY

The following credit transactions all took place on 31 Jan and have been entered into the purchase returns daybook of Thomas & Tilly as shown below. No entries have yet been made in the ledgers.

Purchase returns daybook

Date 20XX	Details	Credit note number	Total £	VAT £	Net £
31 Jan	May Ltd	230C	1,920	320	1,600
31 Jan	Hammond & Co	231C	1,200	200	1,000
	Totals		**3,120**	520	2,600

(a) **What will be the entries in the payables ledger?**

Payables ledger

Account name	Amount £	Debit ✓	Credit ✓

Picklist: Net, Purchases, Payables ledger control, May Ltd, Purchases returns, Sales, Receivables ledger control, Sales returns, VAT, Hammond & Co, Total.

(b) **What will be the entries in the general ledger?**

General ledger

Account name	Amount £	Debit ✓	Credit ✓

Picklist: May Ltd, Net, Purchases, Payables ledger control, Purchases returns, Sales, Receivables ledger control, Sales returns, Hammond & Co, Total, VAT

80 FINCH'S

The following transactions all took place on 31 Dec and have been entered into the sales daybook of Finch's as shown below. No entries have yet been made into the ledger system.

Date 20XX	Details	Invoice number	Total £	VAT £	Net £
31 Dec	Lou and Phil's	700	5,040	840	4,200
31 Dec	Eddie and Co	701	10,560	1,760	8,800
31 Dec	Noah's Arc	702	2,880	480	2,400
31 Dec	Alex and Freddie	703	720	120	600
	Totals		19,200	3,200	16,000

(a) **What will be the entries in the subsidiary (memorandum) ledger for receivables?**

Account name	Amount £	Debit ✓	Credit ✓

Picklist: Lou and Phil's, Eddie and Co, Noah's Arc, Alex and Freddie, Purchases, Payables ledger control, Purchases returns, Sales, Receivables ledger control, Sales returns, VAT

(b) **What will be the entries in the general ledger?**

Account name	Amount £	Debit ✓	Credit ✓

Picklist: Payables ledger control, Sales, Receivables ledger control, Sales returns, VAT

81 JESSICA & CO

The following credit transactions all took place on 31 Dec and have been entered into the purchases returns daybook as shown below. No entries have yet been made in the ledgers.

Purchases returns daybook

Date 20XX	Details	Credit note number	Total £	VAT £	Net £
31 Dec	Iona Ltd	4763	1,680	280	1,400
31 Dec	Matilda Ltd	2164	4,320	720	3,600
	Totals		6,000	1,000	5,000

(a) **What will be the entries in the payables ledger?**

Payables ledger

Account name	Amount £	Debit ✓	Credit ✓

Picklist: Iona Ltd, Matilda Ltd, Net, Purchases, Payables ledger control, Purchases returns, Sales, Receivables ledger control, Sales returns, Total, VAT

(b) **What will be the entries in the general ledger?**

General ledger

Account name	Amount £	Debit ✓	Credit ✓

Picklist: Iona Ltd, Matilda Ltd, Net, Purchases, Payables ledger control, Purchases returns, Sales, Receivables ledger control, Sales returns, VAT, Total

82 HORSEY REACH

The following transactions all took place on 31 July and have been entered into the discounts allowed daybook of Horsey Reach as shown below. No entries have yet been made into the ledger system.

Date 20XX	Details	Credit note number	Total £	VAT £	Net £
31 July	Ashleigh Buildings	145	36.00	6.00	30.00
31 July	143 WGT	146	54.00	9.00	45.00
31 July	McDuff McGregor	147	43.20	7.20	36.00
31 July	Cameron Travel	148	93.60	15.60	78.00
	Totals		**226.80**	**37.80**	**189.00**

(a) **What will be the entries in the general ledger?**

Account name	Amount £	Debit ✓	Credit ✓

Picklist: 13 WGT, Ashleigh Buildings, Cameron Travel, Discounts Allowed, Discounts Received, McDuff McGregor, Purchases, Payables ledger control, Sales, Receivables ledger control, VAT

(b) **What will be the entries in the subsidiary ledger?**

Account name	Amount £	Debit ✓	Credit ✓

Picklist: 143 WGT, Ashleigh Buildings, Cameron Travel, Discounts Allowed, Discounts Received, McDuff McGregor, Purchases, Payables ledger control, Sales, Receivables ledger control, VAT

83   BUTTERFLY BEES

These are the totals from the discounts received book of Butterfly Bees at the end of the month.

Total £	VAT £	Net £
427.20	71.20	356.00

(a)   What will be the entries in the general ledger?

Account name	Amount £	Debit ✓	Credit ✓

One of the entries in the discounts received daybook is for a credit note received from Bella Bumps for £20 plus VAT.

(b)   What will be the entry in the payables ledger?

Account name	Amount £	Debit ✓	Credit ✓

84   OLIVIA ROSE BRIDAL SUPPLIES

These are the totals from the discounts allowed book of Olivia Rose Bridal Supplies at the end of the month.

Total £	VAT £	Net £
226.80	37.80	189.00

(a)   What will be the entries in the general ledger?

Account name	Amount £	Debit ✓	Credit ✓

One of the entries in the discounts allowed daybook is for a credit note sent to Bridezilla for £45 plus VAT.

(b)   What will be the entry in the receivables ledger?

Account name	Amount £	Debit ✓	Credit ✓

85 SUSSEX TRADING

These are the totals of the discounts allowed daybook of Sussex Trading at the end of the month.

Total £	VAT £	Net £
492.00	82.00	410.00

(a) **What will be the entries in the general ledger?**

Account name	Amount £	Debit ✓	Credit ✓

One of the entries is for a credit note sent to Woody Woodburn for £65 plus VAT.

(b) **What will be the entry in the subsidiary ledger for receivables?**

Account name	Amount £	Debit ✓	Credit ✓

86 ROXY CAKE DESIGNS

These are the totals of the discounts allowed daybook of Roxy Cake Designs at the end of the month.

Total £	VAT £	Net £
381.60	63.60	318.00

(a) **What will be the entries in the general ledger?**

Account name	Amount £	Debit ✓	Credit ✓

One of the entries is for a credit note sent to Percy Tran for £28 plus VAT.

(b) **What will be the entry in the receivables ledger?**

Account name	Amount £	Debit ✓	Credit ✓

87 ANNANDALE SUPPLIES

These are the totals of the purchases returns daybook of Annandale Supplies at the end of the month.

Total £	VAT £	Net £
5,496.00	916.00	4,580.00

(a) **Show the correct entries to be made in the general ledger by entering the correct account name and debit or credit next to each amount.**

Account name	Amount £	Debit/Credit
	4,580.00	
	916.00	
	5,496.00	

Picklist: Purchases / Sales / Sales returns / Purchases returns / Bank / VAT /Payables ledger control / Receivables ledger control / Debit / Credit

These are the totals of the sales returns daybook of Annandale Supplies at the end of the month.

Total £	VAT £	Net £
3,001.20	500.20	2,501.00

(b) **Show the correct entries to be made in the general ledger by entering the correct account name and debit or credit next to each amount.**

Account name	Amount £	Debit/Credit
	2,501.00	
	500.20	
	3,001.20	

Picklist: Purchases / Sales / Sales returns / Purchases returns / Bank / VAT /Payables ledger control / Receivables ledger control / Debit / Credit

88   NC CLEANING SUPPLIES

These are the totals from the purchases returns daybook of NC Cleaning Supplies at the end of the month.

Total £	VAT £	Net £
318.00	53.00	265.00

(a)   Show the entries to be made in the general ledger by selecting the correct account name and debit or credit option against each amount. You may use each option more than once.

Account name	Amount £	Debit/Credit
	318.00	
	53.00	
	265.00	

Options: Purchases, Payables ledger control, Purchases returns, Sales, Receivables ledger control, Sales returns, VAT, Debit, Credit

These are the totals from the sales returns daybook of NC Cleaning Supplies at the end of the month.

Total £	VAT £	Net £
180.00	30.00	150.00

(b)   Show the entries to be made in the general ledger by selecting the correct account name and debit or credit option against each amount. You may use each option more than once.

Account name	Amount £	Debit/Credit
	150.00	
	30.00	
	180.00	

Options: Purchases, Payables ledger control, Purchases returns, Sales, Receivables ledger control, Sales returns, VAT, Debit, Credit

89   CHUGGER LTD

The following transactions all took place on 31 July and have been entered in the credit side of the cash book as shown below. No entries have yet been made in the ledgers.

Cash book – Credit side

Date 20XX	Details	VAT £	Bank £
31 July	Stationery	16	96
31 July	Photocopier repair	40	240

(a)   **What will be the entries in the general ledger?**

General ledger

Account name	Amount £	Debit ✓	Credit ✓

Picklist: Stationery, Insurance, Repairs, Payables ledger control, Receivables ledger control, VAT

The following transactions all took place on 31 July and have been entered in the debit side of the cash book as shown below. No entries have yet been made in the ledgers.

Cash book – Debit side

Date 20XX	Details	Bank £
31 July	Balance b/f	6,350
31 July	BBG Ltd	7,200
31 July	EFG Ltd	5,000

(b)   **What will be the TWO entries in the receivables ledger?**

Receivables ledger

Account name	Amount £	Debit ✓	Credit ✓

Picklist: Balance b/f, Receivables ledger control, BBG Ltd, Payables ledger control, EFG Ltd, Bank

(c)   **What will be the entry in the general ledger?**

General ledger

Account name	Amount £	Debit ✓	Credit ✓

Picklist: Balance b/f, EFG Ltd Payables ledger control, Receivables ledger control, VAT, Bank, BBG Ltd

90   ITALIAN STALLIONS

The following transactions all took place on 31 Jan and have been entered in the credit side of the cash book of Italian Stallions Ltd as shown below. No entries have yet been made in the ledgers.

Cash book – Credit side

Date 20XX	Details	VAT £	Bank £
31 Jan	Printer repair	32	192
31 Jan	Paper	16	96

(a)   **What will be the entries in the general ledger?**

General ledger

Account name	Amount £	Debit ✓	Credit ✓

Picklist: Repairs, Office supplies, Payables ledger control, Receivables ledger control, VAT

The following transactions all took place on 31 Jan and have been entered in the debit side of the cash book as shown below. No entries have yet been made in the ledgers.

Cash book – Debit side

Date 20XX	Details	Bank £
31 Jan	Balance b/f	5,100
31 Jan	AAG Ltd	4,000
31 Jan	HLG Ltd	3,000

(b)   **What will be the TWO entries in the receivables ledger?**

Receivables ledger

Account name	Amount £	Debit ✔	Credit ✔

Picklist: Balance b/f, Receivables ledger control, AAG Ltd, Payables ledger control, HLG Ltd, Bank

(c)   **What will be the entry in the general ledger?**

General ledger

Account name	Amount £	Debit ✔	Credit ✔

Picklist: Balance b/f, EFG Ltd Payables ledger control, Receivables ledger control, VAT, Bank, BBG Ltd

91   FRED'S FISH

The following transactions all took place on 31 Dec and have been entered in the debit side of the cash book as shown below. No entries have yet been made in the ledgers.

Cash book – Debit side

Date 20XX	Details	Bank £
31 Dec	Balance b/f	4,280
31 Dec	K and D Ltd	8,200

(a)   **What will be the entry in the receivables ledger?**

Receivables ledger

Account name	Amount £	Debit ✔	Credit ✔

Picklist: Balance b/f, Bank, Payables ledger control, K and D Ltd, Receivables ledger control

(b) **What will be the entry in the general ledger?**

General ledger

Account name	Amount £	Debit ✓	Credit ✓

Picklist: Balance b/f, Bank, Payables ledger control, K and D Ltd, Receivables ledger control

The following transactions all took place on 31 Dec and have been entered in the credit side of the cash book as shown below. No entries have yet been made in the ledgers.

Cash book – Credit side

Date 20XX	Details	VAT £	Bank £
31 Dec	Stationery	20	120
31 Dec	Postage		800

(c) **What will be the entries in the general ledger?**

General ledger

Account name	Amount £	Debit ✓	Credit ✓

Picklist: Bank, Postage, Stationery, Payables ledger control, Receivables ledger control, VAT

92 HICKORY HOUSE

Hickory House maintains a petty cash book as both a book of prime entry and part of the double entry accounting system. The following transactions all took place on 31 Dec and have been entered in the petty cash book as shown below. No entries have yet been made in the general ledger.

Petty cash book

Date 20XX	Details	Amount £	Date 20XX	Details	Amount £	VAT £	Postage £	Motor expenses £	Office expenses £
31 Dec	Balance b/f	210.00	31 Dec	Stapler	6.72	1.12			5.60
31 Dec	Bank	90.00	31 Dec	Stamps	15.00		15.00		
			31 Dec	Parking	14.88	2.48		12.40	
			31 Dec	Stationery	19.20	3.20			16.00
			31 Dec	Balance c/d	244.20				
		300.00			300.00	6.80	15.00	12.40	21.60

What will be the FIVE entries in the general ledger?

General ledger

Account name	Amount £	Debit ✓	Credit ✓

Picklist: Balance b/f, Balance c/d, Bank, Stationery, Stapler, Motor expenses, Parking, Office expenses, Petty cash book, Stamps, Postage, VAT

93   MESSI & CO

Messi & Co maintains a petty cash book as a book of prime entry; it is not part of the double entry accounting system. The following transactions all took place on 31 Dec and have been entered in the petty cash book as shown below. No entries have yet been made in the general ledger.

Petty cash book

Date 20XX	Detail	Amount £	Date 20XX	Detail	Amount £	VAT £	Post exps £	Motor exps £	Office exps £
31 Dec	Op bal	100.00	Dec 31	Paper	27.33	4.55			22.78
			31 Dec	Stamps	4.50		4.50		
			31 Dec	Biscuits	6.60	1.10			5.50
			31 Dec	Parking	9.60	1.60		8.00	
			31 Dec	Cl bal	51.97				
		100.00			100.00	7.25	4.50	8.00	28.28

What will be the FIVE entries in the general ledger?

General ledger

Account name	Amount £	Debit ✓	Credit ✓

Picklist: Balance b/f, Balance c/d, Bank, Motor expenses, Paper, Parking, Petty cash control, Office expenses, Petty cash book, Stamps, Postage, VAT

94   STAVROS

Stavros maintains a petty cash book as both a book of prime entry and part of the double entry accounting system. The following transactions all took place on 31 July and have been entered in the petty cash book as shown below. No entries have been made in the general ledger.

Petty cash book

Date 20XX	Details	Amount £	Date 20XX	Details	Amount £	VAT £	Sundry expenses £	Business travel £	Postage
1 July	Balance b/f	140	31 July	Newsagent	16.20	2.70	13.50		
31 July	Bank	110	31 July	Tea & Coffee	60.00	10.00	50.00		
			31 July	Business Travel	36.96	6.16		30.80	
			31 July	Postage	16.00				16.00
			31 July	Balance c/d	120.84				
		250.00			250.00	18.86	63.50	30.80	16.00

What will be the FIVE entries in the general ledger?

General ledger

Account name	Amount £	Debit ✓	Credit ✓

Picklist: Postage, Balance c/d, Bank, Fuel, Balance b/f, Motor repair, Sundry expenses, Petty cash book, VAT, Business Travel

95   YUMMY CUPCAKES

Yummy Cupcakes maintains a petty cash book as a book of prime entry; it is not part of the double entry accounting system. The following transactions all took place on 31 July and have been entered in the petty cash book as shown below. No entries have yet been made in the general ledger.

Petty cash book

Date 20XX	Details	Amount £	Date 20XX	Details	Amount £	VAT £	Sundry expenses £	Business travel £	Postage
1 July	Op balance	150.00	31 July	Parking	15.00	2.50		12.50	
			31 July	Tea & Coffee	12.00	2.00	10.00		
			31 July	Travel	39.44	6.57		32.87	
			31 July	Stamps	4.00				4.00
			31 July	Cl balance	79.56				
		150.00			150.00	11.07	10.00	45.37	4.00

What will be the FIVE entries in the general ledger?

General ledger

Account name	Amount £	Debit ✓	Credit ✓

Picklist: Postage, Balance c/d, Bank, Fuel, Balance b/f, Motor repair, Sundry expenses, Petty cash book, VAT, Business Travel

96 OOH LA!

Ooh La! maintains a petty cash book as both a book of prime entry and part of the double entry accounting system. The following transactions all took place on 31 Jan and have been entered in the petty cash book as shown below. No entries have yet been made in the general ledger.

Petty cash book

Date 20XX	Details	Amount £	Date 20XX	Details	Amount £	VAT £	Sundry expenses £	Motor expense £	Postage
1 Jan	Balance b/f	80.00	31 Jan	Newsagent	12.30		12.30		
31 Jan	Bank	70.00	31 Jan	Post office	43.56	7.26			36.30
			31 Jan	Fuel	20.40	3.40		17.00	
			31 Jan	Tea & Coffee	27.30	4.55	22.75		
			31 Jan	Balance c/d	46.44				
		150.00			150.00	15.21	35.05	17.00	36.30

What will be the FIVE entries in the general ledger?

General ledger

Account name	Amount £	Debit ✓	Credit ✓

Picklist: Postage, Balance c/d, Bank, Motor Expense, Balance b/f, Business Travel, Sundry expenses, Petty cash book, VAT

97   LJ INTERIORS

These are the totals of the petty cash book at the end of the month.

Details	Amount £	Details	Amount £	VAT £	Stationery £	Postage £	Charitable donations £
Total	566	Totals	566	64	320	32	150

What will be the entries in the general ledger?

Account name	Amount £	Debit ✓	Credit ✓

98   KAZ KARATE CLUB

These are the totals of the petty cash book at the end of the month.

Details	Amount £	Details	Amount £	VAT £	Motor expenses £	Postage £	Insurance £
Total	386	Totals	386	31	155	20	180

What will be the entries in the general ledger?

Account name	Amount £	Debit ✓	Credit ✓

99 JACINTA INTERIOR DESIGN

The petty cash at Jacinta Interior Design is restored to £300 at the end of each week. The following amounts were paid out of petty cash during week 22:

Stationery	£42.30 including VAT at 20%
Travelling costs	£76.50
Office refreshments	£38.70
Sundry payables	£72.00 plus VAT at 20%

(a) **Complete the petty cash reimbursement document below to restore the imprest amount of £300.**

Petty cash reimbursement	
Week 22	
Amount required to restore the cash in the petty cash box.	£

(b) **Which one of the following states the entries required to account for the reimbursement to the petty cash float from the bank account?**

A	Dr Petty cash	Cr Bank
B	Dr Bank	Cr Petty cash
C	Dr Drawings	Cr Petty cash
D	Dr Drawings	Cr Bank

100 MARTHA

Martha maintains a petty cash book as both a book of prime entry and part of the double entry accounting system. The petty cash book below has been partly completed for the month of April.

Petty cash book

Date 20XX	Details	Amount £	Date 20XX	Details	Amount £	VAT £	Cleaning expenses £	Motor expenses £	Office expenses £
01 Apr	Bank	150.00	11 Apr	Cleaning supplies	14.88	2.48	12.40		
			12 Apr	Stationery	42.48	7.08			35.40

On 30th April there was one final petty cash payment for the month to be recorded:

Cleaning Services Ltd   £60 including VAT.

(a) **Calculate the VAT and net amounts of this petty cash payment to be recorded in the petty cash book.**

VAT £	Net £

(b)   Calculate the total of the cleaning expense analysis column after taking into consideration the petty cash payment in (a).

£ [   ]

(c)   After taking into consideration the transaction in (a) what will be the entry in the petty cash book to restore to the imprest level of £150.

Details	Amount £	Debit ✓	Credit ✓

Details picklist: Amount, Balance b/d, Balance c/d, Cash from bank

(d)   What is the entry made in the petty cash book to record the closing balance on 30th April?

Details	Amount £	Debit ✓	Credit ✓

Details picklist: Amount, Balance b/d, Balance c/d, Cash from bank

The following petty cash receipts need to be recorded in the petty cash book for the month of May.

98	99	100
Newark Printers	**ERJ Motor Supplies**	**Co-pop**
Printer ink	Wiper blades	Cleaning products
£17.40 including VAT at 20%.	£38.40 inclusive of VAT at 20%.	£6.00 gross of £1.00 VAT.

(e)   For each receipt identify the analysis column to be used for the payment and the amount of the transaction that should be recorded in the analysis column.

Petty cash receipt	Analysis column	Amount £
Newark Printers		
ERJ Motor Supplies		
Co-pop		

Analysis column picklist: Cleaning expenses, Motor expenses, Office expenses

101 ROLAND

The following transactions all took place on 31 July and have been entered into the discounts allowed daybook of Roland as shown below. No entries have yet been made into the ledger system.

Date 20XX	Details	Credit note number	Total £	VAT £	Net £
31 July	Aldo & Co	45	24.00	4.00	20.00
31 July	Hopley Brothers	46	36.00	6.00	30.00
31 July	Fernando's	47	25.20	4.20	21.00
31 July	Richmond Travel	48	38.40	6.40	32.00
	Totals		123.60	20.60	103.00

(a) **What will be the entries in the general ledger?**

Account name	Amount £	Debit ✓	Credit ✓

(b) **What will be the entries in the subsidiary ledger?**

Account name	Amount £	Debit ✓	Credit ✓

102 ROGER

Roger's cash book is both a book of prime entry and part of the double entry bookkeeping system. The following transactions all took place on 31 December and have been entered in the debit side of the cash book as shown below.

Cash book – Debit side

Date 20XX	Details	Cash £	Bank £
31 Dec	Balance b/f	200	2,883
31 Dec	TUV Ltd		4,000

(a)   **What will be the entry in the receivables ledger?**

Receivables ledger

Account name	Amount £	Debit ✔	Credit ✔

(b)   **What will be the entry in the general ledger?**

General ledger

Account name	Amount £	Debit ✔	Credit ✔

The following transactions all took place on 31 December and have been entered in the credit side of the cash book as shown below. No entries have yet been made in the ledgers.

Cash book – Credit side

Date 20XX	Details	VAT £	Cash £	Bank £
31 Dec	Entertainment	32		192
31 Dec	Insurance			240

(c)   **What will be the entries in the general ledger?**

General ledger

Account name	Amount £	Debit ✔	Credit ✔

103   ANDREW, WILLIAM & CO

Below are the totals from the credit side of the cash book at Andrew, William and Co.

Details	Cash	Bank	VAT	Cash purchases	Payables
Totals	3,574.70	10,311.60	869.14	4,345.70	8,671.46

(a)   **Select the correct entries to be made in the general ledger accounts shown below.**

Account name	Amount £	Debit ✔	Credit ✔
Cash purchases			
VAT			
Payables ledger control account			

The purchases and discounts allowed daybooks have been totalled and all amounts have been transferred to the relevant general ledger accounts.

(b)   Identify the correct entries in the payables and receivables ledger.

Daybook	Debit ✓	Credit ✓	Payables ledger ✓	Receivables ledger ✓
Purchases				
Discounts allowed				

104   S WILLIAMS LTD

Below are the totals from the debit side of the cash book at S Williams Ltd.

Details	Cash ✓	Bank ✓	VAT ✓	Cash sales ✓	Receivables ✓
Totals	1,767.36	10,311.24	2,013.10	2,045.60	8,019.90

(a)   Select the correct entries to be made in the general ledger accounts shown below.

Account name	Amount £	Debit ✓	Credit ✓
Cash sales			
VAT			
Receivables ledger control account			

The sales and discounts received daybooks have been totalled and all amounts have been transferred to the relevant general ledger accounts.

(b)   Identify the correct entries in the payables and receivables ledger.

Daybook	Debit ✓	Credit ✓	Payables ledger ✓	Receivables ledger ✓
Sales				
Discounts received				

105   BROOKLYN BOATS

The following two accounts are in the general ledger of Brooklyn Boats at the close of day on 31 Dec.

(a)   **Insert the balance carried down together with date and details.**

(b)   **Insert the totals.**

(c)   **Insert the balance brought down together with date and details.**

Electricity

Date 20XX	Details	Amount £	Date 20XX	Details	Amount £
01 Dec	Balance b/f	870			
12 Dec	Bank	350			
	Total			Total	

Picklist: Balance b/d, Balance c/d, Bank, Closing balance, Opening balance, Payables ledger control

Discounts received

Date 20XX	Details	Amount £	Date 20XX	Details	Amount £
			1 Dec	Bal b/f	500
			15 Dec	Payables ledger control	100
	Total			Total	

Picklist: Balance b/d, Balance c/d, Bank, Closing balance, Opening balance, Receivables ledger control

106 WIGGLE POGGLE LTD

The following two accounts are in the general ledger of Wiggle Poggle Ltd at the close of day on 31 July.

(a) **Insert the balance carried down together with date and details.**

(b) **Insert the totals.**

(c) **Insert the balance brought down together with date and details.**

Discount allowed

Date 20XX	Details	Amount £	Date 20XX	Details	Amount £
01 July	Balance b/f	1,560			
14 July	Receivables ledger control account	480			
16 July	Receivables ledger control account	120			
	Total			**Total**	

Picklist: Balance b/d, Balance c/d, Bank, Closing balance, Opening balance, Receivables ledger control

Interest income

Date 20XX	Details	Amount £	Date 20XX	Details	Amount £
			01 July	Balance b/f	320
			28 July	Bank	80
	Total			**Total**	

Picklist: Balance b/d, Balance c/d, Bank, Closing balance, Opening balance, Receivables ledger control

107 CRAZY CURTAINS

The following two accounts are in the general ledger of Crazy Curtains at the close of day on 31 Jan.

(a) Insert the balance carried down together with date and details.

(b) Insert the totals.

(c) Insert the balance brought down together with date and details.

Electricity expense

Date 20XX	Details	Amount £	Date 20XX	Details	Amount £
01 Jan	Bal b/f	200			
22 Jan	Bank	250			
	Total			Total	

Picklist: Balance b/d, Balance c/d, Bank, Closing balance, Opening balance, Electricity Expense

Rental income

Date 20XX	Details	Amount £	Date 20XX	Details	Amount £
			01 Jan	Balance b/f	400
			28 Jan	Bank	600
	Total			Total	

Picklist: Balance b/d, Balance c/d, Bank, Closing balance, Opening balance, Receivables ledger control

108 BALANCES 1

The following four accounts are in the general ledger at close of day on 31 December.

Capital

Date 20XX	Details	Amount £	Date 20XX	Details	Amount £
			01 Dec	Balance b/f	5,000
			25 Dec	Bank	1,000

Fixtures and Fittings

Date 20XX	Details	Amount £	Date 20XX	Details	Amount £
01 Dec	Balance b/f	18,500	8 Dec	Journal	1,200
12 Dec	Bank	2,500			

Loan

Date 20XX	Details	Amount £	Date 20XX	Details	Amount £
31 Dec	Bank	1,650	01 Dec	Balance b/f	24,880

Drawings

Date 20XX	Details	Amount £	Date 20XX	Details	Amount £
01 Dec	Balance b/f	1,800			
20 Dec	Bank	650			

Record the totals and balances of each account in the table below by:

- inserting the balance carried down at 31 December,

- showing whether the balance carried down will be a debit or a credit, and

- inserting the total that will be shown in both the debit and credit columns after the account has been balanced.

Account name	Balance c/d at 31 December £	Debit/Credit	Total shown in both the debit and credit columns £
Capital			
Fixtures and Fittings			
Loan			
Drawings			

109 BALANCES 2

The following four accounts are in the general ledger at close of day on 31 March.

Capital

Date 20XX	Details	Amount £	Date 20XX	Details	Amount £
			01 Mar	Balance b/f	10,000
			25 Mar	Bank	5,000

Plant and Machinery

Date 20XX	Details	Amount £	Date 20XX	Details	Amount £
01 Mar	Balance b/f	8,500	8 Mar	Journal	800
12 Mar	Bank	1,250			

Loan

Date 20XX	Details	Amount £	Date 20XX	Details	Amount £
31 Mar	Bank	1,020	01 Mar	Balance b/f	15,200

Drawings

Date 20XX	Details	Amount £	Date 20XX	Details	Amount £
01 Mar	Balance b/f	3,330			
20 Mar	Bank	890			

Record the totals and balances of each account in the table below by:

- inserting the balance carried down at 31 March,

- showing whether the balance carried down will be a debit or a credit, and

- inserting the total that will be shown in both the debit and credit columns after the account has been balanced.

Account name	Balance c/d at 31 March £	Debit/Credit	Total shown in both the debit and credit columns £
Capital			
Plant and Machinery			
Loan			
Drawings			

110 BALANCES 3

The following accounts are in the general ledger at 31 December.

AD014

Date 20XX	Details	Amount £	Date 20XX	Details	Amount £
21 Dec	Bank	465	14 Dec	Cash	947
28 Dec	Bank	1,987			

AD019

Date 20XX	Details	Amount £	Date 20XX	Details	Amount £
19 Dec	Cash	136	3 Dec	Bank	948
			12 Dec	Cash	2,362

AD036

Date 20XX	Details	Amount £	Date 20XX	Details	Amount £
7 Dec	Cash	754	3 Dec	Bank	856
18 Dec	Bank	429	27 Dec	Cash	306

(a) Identify the entries required to record the balance carried down in each account.

Account	Amount £	Debit ✓	Credit ✓
AD014			
AD019			
AD036			

The following ledger account is ready to be totalled and balanced at the end of December.

(b) Complete the account below by inserting the following entries into the account:

- The balance carried down as at 31 December

- The totals (you may use each total more than once)

- The balance brought down as at 1 January

Receivables

Date	Details	Amount £	Date	Details	Amount £
1 Dec	Balance brought down	9,864	17 Dec	Cash	7,493
21 Dec	Sales	4,928			

Entries		
	Total	14,792
1 Jan	Balance carried down	7,299
31 Dec	Balance brought down	7,299

Section 2

ANSWERS TO PRACTICE QUESTIONS

UNDERSTAND HOW TO SET UP BOOKKEEPING SYSTEMS

1   **LEO LTD**

(a)

General ledger code	GL530
Customer account code	DEF14

(b)

To help trace orders and amounts due from particular customers

2   **ELLA'S PAINTS**

(a)

General ledger code	GL395
Supplier account code	MEG20

(b)

To help trace orders and amounts due to particular suppliers

3   **ROBERTO & CO**

(a)

Supplier account code	ALE1
General ledger code	GL72

(b)

To help calculate expense incurred in a GL account

4 ACCOUNTING EQUATION 1

(a)

Item	True/False
Assets less capital is equal to liabilities	True
Assets plus liabilities are equal to capital	False
Capital plus liabilities are equal to assets	True

(b)

Item	Asset or liability?
Inventory	Asset
Machinery	Asset
5 year loan	Liability

5 CLASSIFICATION

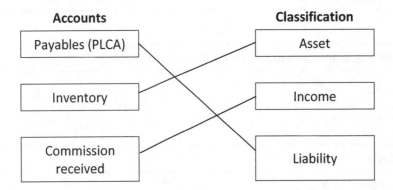

Accounts	Classification
Payables (PLCA)	Asset
Inventory	Income
Commission received	Liability

6 ACCOUNTING EQUATION 2

(a)

Item	True/False
Capital is equal to assets plus liabilities	False
Assets less liabilities are equal to capital	True
Liabilities are equal to capital plus assets	False

(b)

Item	Asset or liability?
VAT owed to tax authorities	Liability
Amounts owing to payables	Liability
Money in the bank	Asset

7 CAPEX

Item	Capital income	Revenue income	Capital expenditure	Revenue expenditure
Receipt from sale of motor vehicle	✓			
Receipts from credit sales		✓		
Purchase of machinery			✓	
Payment of electricity bill				✓
Purchase of goods for resale				✓

8 REVEX

Item	Capital income	Revenue income	Capital expenditure	Revenue expenditure
Receipt from sale of machinery	✓			
Payment of telephone bill				✓
Purchase of building			✓	
Receipts from cash sales		✓		
Receipts from receivables		✓		

9 EXPENDITURE TYPES

Item	Capital expenditure	Revenue expenditure	Capital income	Revenue income
Purchase of a new computer system	✓			
Receipts from customers				✓
Receipt from sale of fixtures and fittings			✓	
Payments of salaries to staff		✓		
Purchase of cleaning materials		✓		
Receipt of bank interest				✓

10   ASSET OR LIABILITY

(a)

Item	Asset or liability?
Factory building	Asset
Money due to suppliers	Liability
Car used in the business	Asset

(b)   The expense electricity will **increase**; the asset of bank will **decrease**.

11   ACCOUNTING EQUATION 3

Assets £	Liabilities £	Capital £
158,360	28,870	129,490

12   MULTIPLE CHOICE 1

(a)

		Capital expenditure or revenue expense
(i)	Work to install additional, high-specification, electrical power cabling and circuits so that additional plant and equipment can become operational	Capital
(ii)	Replacement of some loose and damaged roof tiles following a recent storm	Revenue
(iii)	Repainting the factory administration office	Revenue
(iv)	Modifications to the factory entrance to enable a large item of plant and equipment to be installed	Capital

(b)   **C**   It is a summary of assets, liabilities and equity at a specified date

(c)   **Debit balances:**   **Credit balances:**

   C   Assets and expenses   Liabilities, capital and revenues

13   MULTIPLE CHOICE 2

(a)   **D**   It is a summary of income and expenditure for an accounting period

(b)   **D**   Assets and expenses normally have debit balances

(c)   **B**   A debit balance exists where the total of debit entries is less than the total of credit entries

14   LEO

(a)

	TRANSACTION	CASH	CREDIT
(i)	Receipt of goods worth £140.59 from a supplier together with an invoice for that amount.		✓
(ii)	Payment of £278.50 by cheque for a purchase at the till.	✓	
(iii)	Receipt of a deposit of £15.00 for goods.	✓	
(iv)	Sending of an invoice for £135.00 to the payer of the deposit for the remaining value of the goods.		✓
(v)	Sale of goods for £14.83, payment received by credit card.	✓	

(b)   (i)   Asset – inventory

(ii)   Expense

(iii)   Income

(iv)   Asset – trade receivables

(v)   Expense

(vi)   Liability (this is a special liability known as capital)

(vii)   Liability – payables

(viii)   Asset

(ix)   Asset

(x)   Income

(xi)   Asset

15   ACCOUNT CODES

(a)

Date	Customer name	Customer account code
1 August	Worthington Ltd	CWORT092
4 August	Moss Plc	CMOSS093

Date	Supplier name	Supplier account code
2 August	Morley & Sons	SMORL076
5 August	Chapman Ltd	SCHAP077

(b)

Statement	True ✓	False ✓
The reconciliation between the individual payables ledger and the control account is completed automatically	✓	
General ledger accounts need to be manually balanced off to extract a trial balance		✓

(c)

Consequence	✓
The total sales value will be understated	✓
The business may despatch goods that have not been sold	
The total amount owed to payables will be understated	
The business may be paid for goods that have not been sold	
The business may pay the incorrect amount to a supplier	
The business will receive more money from a customer than they are expecting per their customer report	✓

Feedback:

Item 1: Sales would have been debited rather than credited resulting in understatement. Item 2: Goods are despatched on generation of a sales order, not an invoice or credit note. Item 3: Errors over sales affects receivables rather than payables. Item 4: The business should be paid the right amount as a sales invoice was correctly sent to the customer. Item 5: The transaction invoices sales rather than purchases. Item 6: The business will have understated receivables and as a result will be paid more than they expect.

(d)

Summarising the transactions for a period and classifying them into relevant categories of income and expenditure to show the overall profit or loss for the period	Statement of profit or loss
Detailing all of the transactions with a credit customer during the period and advising a credit customer of the balance outstanding on their account	Supplier statement
To summarise the balances on each of the general ledger accounts in order to begin the preparation of the financial statements	Trial balance
To correct an invoice that has been prepared incorrectly by overstating the value of goods supplied	Credit note

16   PRINCIPLES 1

(a)

Assets £	Liabilities £	Capital £
£21,236.90	£9,929.45	£11,307.45

Feedback:

Assets = £10,180.00 + £4,367.45 + £2,100.00 + £4,589.45 = £21,236.90

Liabilities = £8,392.48 + £1,536.97 = £9,929.45

Capital = Assets − Liabilities = £21,236.90 − £9,929.45 = £11,307.45

(b)

Transaction 1	
Effect	✓
Increase assets	✓
Decrease assets	
Increase capital	
Increase liabilities	✓
Decrease liabilities	

Transaction 2	
Effect	✓
Increase liabilities	
Increase capital	✓
Decrease capital	
Increase assets	✓
Decrease liabilities	

Feedback:

Transaction 1 – Dr Non-current assets, Cr Payables

Transaction 2 – Dr Cash, Cr Inventory, Cr Capital

Note: the increase in cash will exceed the reduction in inventory as the goods were sold at a profit.

(c)

Account balance	Debit ✓	Credit ✓
Opening inventory	✓	
Payables		✓
Drawings	✓	

17 DIGITAL BOOKKEEPING

(a)

Details	Ledger code		Details	Ledger code
Sales – dog food	2019		Insurance expense	3072
Sales – dog bedding	2020		Courier expense	3073
Sales – dog toys	2021		Advertising expense	3074

Feedback: As these are new general ledger codes, we can assume they will run in sequence from the first ones given in the question.

(b)

Coding system	✓
Alphanumerical	
Alphabetical	
Numerical	✓

Feedback: only numbers are used in the coding system.

(c)

Consequence	✓
Assets will be understated	✓
Sales will be understated	
Purchases will be understated	
Expenses will be overstated	✓

(d)

Statement	True ✓	False ✓
It is not possible to post a duplicate transaction using a digital bookkeeping system		✓
Digital bookkeeping systems can automatically post recurring entries	✓	
The trial balance will automatically balance using a digital bookkeeping system	✓	

Feedback:

Item 1 – the operator could post the same transaction into the system twice. Item 2 – this is a typical function of digital systems. Item 3 – Digital systems will always process matching debits and credits although may use a suspense account.

18 PRINCIPLES 2

(a)

Item	
Motor vehicles	Assets
Insurance costs	Expenses
Drawings	Capital
Payables	Liabilities

(b)

Transaction	Dual effect 1	Dual effect 2
Owner invests £20,000 cash into the business bank account	Increases assets	Increases capital
Purchases a laptop computer for use within the business, paying in cash	Increases assets	Decreases assets
Makes a sale to a customer realising a profit on the sale. Customer agrees to pay at a later date	Increases capital	Increases assets
Owner withdraws £10,000 cash from the business to pay for a private holiday	Decreases assets	Decreases capital
A credit customer pays the amount owed	Increases assets	Decreases assets

Feedback: Item 1 – This is capital introduced. Item 2 – Non-current assets increase, but cash reduces by an equivalent amount. Item 3 – Trade receivables increase by more than the reduction in inventory (as a profit has been made). Item 4 – Cash decreases and the drawings also result in a decrease in capital. Item 5 – Cash increases and trade receivables decrease by an equivalent amount.

(c)

£	3,300.00

Feedback: Assets – liabilities = Capital

Office equipment + £4,593.90 + £1,342.80 + £1030.00 – £6,780.00 = £3,486.70

Rearrange the equation:

Office equipment = £3,486.70 – £4,593.90 – £1,342.80 – £1030.00 + £6,780.00 = £3,300.00

19 PRINCIPLES 3

(a)

Item	Capital expenditure	Revenue expenditure	Capital income	Revenue income
Purchase of computer equipment	✓			
Receipts from credit sales				✓
Receipt from sale of motor vehicle (non-current asset)			✓	
Purchase of motor vehicle	✓			
Purchase of stationery		✓		
Payment of rent		✓		

(b)

Statement	True ✓	False ✓
Assets less liabilities are equal to capital	✓	
The business and owner are treated as two separate entities	✓	
A debit increases an item of income		✓

(c)

Item	Option
Computer equipment	Assets
Petty cash	Assets
Money owed to suppliers	Liabilities

PROCESS CUSTOMER TRANSACTIONS

20   ALESSANDRO LTD

(a)

Alessandro Ltd **8 Alan Street** **Glasgow, G1 7DJ** **VAT Registration No. 398 2774 01**					
Palermo Wholesale 167 Front St Stanley DH8 4TJ **Invoice No:** 327			**Customer account code:** AGG42 **Delivery note number: 24369** **Date:** 1 Aug 20XX		
Quantity	**Product code**	**Total list price** **£**	**Net amount after discount** **£**	**VAT** **£**	**Gross** **£**
40	SB05	2,500	2,200	440	2,640

(b)

Prompt payment discount

21   HLB WHOLESALE

(a)

Painting Supplies Ltd **19 Edmund St** **Newcastle, NE6 5DJ** **VAT Registration No. 402 2958 02**					
HLB Wholesale 98 Back St Consett DH4 3PD **Date:** 1 Feb 20XX			**Customer account code:** HLB24 **Delivery note number: 46589** **Invoice No:** 298		
Quantity	**Product code**	**Total list price** **£**	**Net amount after discount** **£**	**VAT** **£**	**Gross** **£**
20	SD19	300	270	54	324

(b)

Trade discount

22   MASHED LTD

(a)

Hickory House						
22 Nursery Road						
Keighley, BD22 7BD						
VAT Registration No. 476 1397 02						

Mashed Ltd
42 Moorside Court
Ilkley
Leeds, LS29 4PR

Customer account code: MA87

Delivery note number: 472

Date: 1 Aug 20XX

Invoice No: 47

Quantity of pots	Product code	Total list price £	Net amount after discount £	VAT £	Gross £
20	P10	100	90	18	108

(b)

Bulk discount

23   ROCKY RICARDO

(a)

Rocky Ricardo					
1 Rocky Way					
Middleton, M42 5TU					
VAT Registration No. 298 3827 04					

Alpha Group
Alpha House
Warwick
WR11 5TB

Customer account code: ALP01

Delivery note number: 2132

Date: 1 Dec 20XX

Invoice No: 950

Quantity of cases	Product code	Total list price £	Net amount after discount £	VAT £	Gross £
200	A1	2,000	1,800	360	2,160

(b)

Sales daybook

Date 20XX	Details	Invoice No:	Total £	VAT £	Net £
1 Dec	Alpha Group	950	2,160	360	1,800

(c)

Invoice 189

(d) **(i)**

£594

(ii)

£600

24 SDB

Sales daybook

Date 20XX	Details	Invoice number	Total £	VAT £	Net £	Sales type 1 £	Sales type 2 £
31 Dec	Poonams	105	3,600	600	3,000		3,000
31 Dec	D. Taylor	106	7,680	1,280	6,400	6,400	
31 Dec	Smiths	107	3,840	640	3,200		3,200
	Totals		15,120	2,520	12,600	6,400	6,200

25 MAHINDRA LTD

Sales daybook

Date 20XX	Details	Invoice number	Total £	VAT £	Net £	Sales type 1 £	Sales type 2 £
31 Jan	Square Ltd	3567	1,200	200	1,000	1,000	
31 Jan	Oval & Co	3568	9,600	1,600	8,000		8,000
31 Jan	Diamond Ltd	3569	13,200	2,200	11,000		11,000
31 Jan	Triangle Ltd	3570	7,920	1,320	6,600	6,600	
	Totals		31,920	5,320	26,600	7,600	19,000

26   PAR FOR THE COURSE GOLF SUPPLIES

(a)

Discount type	✓
Prompt payment	
Trade	
Bulk	✓

Feedback: Remember that bulk discount relates to discount given by a supplier for sales orders above a certain quantity.

(b)

	£
Net amount after discounts	2,685.00
VAT @ 20%	537.00
Total	3,222.00

Feedback: Net amount = (300 × £5) + (150 × £7.90) = £2,685

(c)

Menu option	✓
Purchases daybook	
Purchase returns daybook	
Cash book	
Sales daybook	✓
Sales returns daybook	
Discounts allowed daybook	
Discounts received daybook	

Date	Customer code	Customer	General ledger code	Invoice number	Net £	VAT code
13 Aug	EREH094	Erehwon Golf Club	Option 1	2808	2,685.00	Option 2

Option 1	✓		Option 2	✓
1001 Sales – golf equipment	✓		V0 – 0%	
1002 Sales – golf buggies			V5 – 5%	
4001 Purchases – golf equipment			V20 – 20%	✓
7001 Receivables				

27 LINKEES TOY MAKERS LTD

(a)

Discount type	✓
Prompt payment	✓
Trade	
Bulk	

(b)

	£
Net amount after discounts	675.00
VAT @ 20%	135.00
Total	810.00

(c)

Menu option	✓
Purchases daybook	
Purchase returns daybook	
Cash book	
Sales daybook	✓
Sales returns daybook	
Discounts allowed daybook	
Discounts received daybook	

Date	Customer code	Customer	General ledger code	Invoice number	Net £	VAT code
17 May	THOM08	Thomas' Toys	Option 1	2808	675.00	Option 2

Option 1	✓
1001 Sales – toys	
1002 Sales – board games	✓
4001 Purchases – Inventory	
7001 Receivables	

Option 2	✓
V0 – 0%	
V5 – 5%	
V20 – 20%	✓
V1 – Exempt	

28   WILLIAM & SAMMY LTD

(a)

Sales invoice 286

(b)

£4,481.28

(c)

£4,668.00

29   DIAMONDS & RUBIES LTD

<table>
<tr><td colspan="4" align="center">Stavros
121 Baker St
Newcastle, NE1 7DJ</td></tr>
<tr><td colspan="2">To: Diamonds & Rubies Ltd</td><td colspan="2" align="right">Date: 31 Aug 20XX</td></tr>
<tr><td>Date 20XX</td><td>Details</td><td align="center">Transaction amount
£</td><td align="center">Outstanding amount
£</td></tr>
<tr><td>5 Aug</td><td>Invoice 3927</td><td align="center">4,640</td><td align="center">4,640</td></tr>
<tr><td>10 Aug</td><td>Credit note 96</td><td align="center">980</td><td align="center">3,660</td></tr>
<tr><td>21 Aug</td><td>Invoice 3964</td><td align="center">1,560</td><td align="center">5,220</td></tr>
<tr><td>28 Aug</td><td>Credit note 104</td><td align="center">650</td><td align="center">4,570</td></tr>
<tr><td>30 Aug</td><td>Cheque received</td><td align="center">2,100</td><td align="center">2,470</td></tr>
</table>

30   MAX LTD

<table>
<tr><td colspan="4" align="center">Painting Supplies Ltd
19 Edmund St
Newcastle, NE6 5DJ</td></tr>
<tr><td colspan="2">To: Max Ltd</td><td colspan="2" align="right">Date: 28 Feb 20XX</td></tr>
<tr><td>Date 20XX</td><td>Details</td><td align="center">Transaction amount
£</td><td align="center">Outstanding amount
£</td></tr>
<tr><td>5 Feb</td><td>Invoice 4658</td><td align="center">2,560</td><td align="center">2,560</td></tr>
<tr><td>11 Feb</td><td>Invoice 3964</td><td align="center">3,290</td><td align="center">5,850</td></tr>
<tr><td>21 Feb</td><td>Credit note 125</td><td align="center">230</td><td align="center">5,620</td></tr>
<tr><td>23 Feb</td><td>Credit note 139</td><td align="center">560</td><td align="center">5,060</td></tr>
<tr><td>27 Feb</td><td>Cheque received</td><td align="center">1,900</td><td align="center">3,160</td></tr>
</table>

31 BETA BOARDS

<table>
<tr><td colspan="4" style="text-align:center">Beta Boards
3 Victoria Avenue
Troon
KA5 2BD</td></tr>
<tr><td colspan="2">To: Ava Ltd</td><td colspan="2">Date: 31 Aug 20XX</td></tr>
<tr><td>Date 20XX</td><td>Details</td><td>Transaction amount £</td><td>Outstanding amount £</td></tr>
<tr><td>10 Aug</td><td>Invoice 222</td><td>350</td><td>350</td></tr>
<tr><td>12 Aug</td><td>Cheque</td><td>225</td><td>125</td></tr>
<tr><td>15 Aug</td><td>Invoice 305</td><td>744</td><td>869</td></tr>
<tr><td>20 Aug</td><td>Credit note 194</td><td>339</td><td>530</td></tr>
<tr><td>24 Aug</td><td>Cheque</td><td>530</td><td>0</td></tr>
</table>

32 BELLA PUMPKIN

(a) – (b)

Bella Pumpkin

Date 20XX	Details	Amount £	Date 20XX	Details	Amount £
12 Dec	Invoice 1001	1,700	21 Dec	Credit note 101	940
21 Dec	Invoice 1004	2,350	29 Dec	Cheque rec'd	2,000
27 Dec	Invoice 1010	470	31 Dec	Balance c/d	1,580
		4,520			**4,520**
20XY 1 Jan	Balance b/d	1,580			

(c)

<table>
<tr><td colspan="4" style="text-align:center">Rocky Ricardo
1 Rocky Way
Middleton, M42 5TU</td></tr>
<tr><td colspan="2">To: Bella Pumpkin</td><td colspan="2">Date: 31 Dec 20XX</td></tr>
<tr><td>Date 20XX</td><td>Details</td><td>Transaction amount £</td><td>Outstanding amount £</td></tr>
<tr><td>12 Dec</td><td>Invoice 1001</td><td>1,700</td><td>1,700</td></tr>
<tr><td>21 Dec</td><td>Invoice 1004</td><td>2,350</td><td>4,050</td></tr>
<tr><td>21 Dec</td><td>Credit note 101</td><td>940</td><td>3,110</td></tr>
<tr><td>27 Dec</td><td>Invoice 1010</td><td>470</td><td>3,580</td></tr>
<tr><td>29 Dec</td><td>Cheque</td><td>2,000</td><td>1,580</td></tr>
</table>

33   HENRY LTD

(a)

Transaction type	Date	Details	Amount £	Action
Balance b/f	1 Aug 20XX		473.87	Allocate full amount – 1028
Invoice 1046	4 Aug 20XX	Goods	1,059.60	Query underpayment
Invoice 1059	9 Aug 20XX	Services	462.20	Query overpayment
Invoice 1068	10 Aug 20XX	Goods	789.48	Allocate full amount – 1086
Invoice 1096	14 Aug 20XX	Goods	662.20	Allocate full amount – 1096

Feedback:

Balance b/f – This amount matches the amount remitted against Invoice 1028.

Invoice 1046 – The amount remitted of £1,006.62 is £1,059.60 less 5% settlement discount. However, the invoice was settled 12 days after it was raised so the discount should not have been taken.

Invoice 1059 – The amount remitted of £462.20 is equivalent to the amount of the invoice. However, this was paid within 7 days so qualifies for the settlement discount.

Invoice 1068 – The amount remitted of £789.48 is equivalent to the amount of the invoice which does not qualify for a settlement discount as paid after 12 days.

Invoice 1096 – The amount remitted of £629.09 is equivalent to the amount of the invoice less settlement discount which it qualifies for as paid within 10 days of the invoice date.

(b)

Customer name	Invoice number	Amount before discount £	Amount after prompt payment discount £
Oliver John & Co	387	8,345.60	7,928.32
Excelsior Ltd	395	4,562.40	4,334.28

(c)

Customer name	Prompt payment Discount %	Invoice amount £	Amount paid £	Amount that should have been paid £	Amount outstanding £
Galahad	5	7,529.40	7,093.52	7,152.93	59.41

Feedback: The correct payment is £7,529.40 × 95% = £7,152.93

34   KLOPP & CO

(a)

Transaction type	Date	Details	Amount £	Action
Balance b/f	1 Apr 20XX		752.34	Allocate full amount – 342
Invoice 354	2 Apr 20XX	Goods	475.61	Allocate full amount – 354
Invoice 362	9 Apr 20XX	Services	834.25	Query underpayment
Invoice 371	12 Apr 20XX	Services	245.50	Allocate full amount – 371
Invoice 379	13 Apr 20XX	Goods	1,051.34	Allocate full amount – 379
Credit note 46	14 Apr 20XX	Correction – 379	178.72	Allocate full amount – CN46
Invoice 383	14 Apr 20XX	Goods	649.23	Allocate full amount – 383
Invoice 391	19 Apr 20XX	Goods	507.75	Allocate full amount – 391

Feedback: Invoice 362 – It appears that the customer has taken the prompt payment discount of 4%, but it has been paid after 8 days. Invoice 371 – As this invoice was paid after 5 days a prompt payment discount has been taken resulting in a payment of £245.50 × 96% = £235.68. Invoice 379 & C/N 46 – This invoice did not qualify for a prompt payment discount. Invoice 379 and the credit note amount to a net payment due of £1,051.34 – £178.72 = £872.62. This is exactly what has been remitted. Invoice 391 – As this invoice was paid after 5 days a prompt payment discount has been taken resulting in a payment of £507.75 × 96% = £487.44.

(b)

Reason	✓
The customer has taken a prompt payment discount of 6% that they were not entitled to, on an invoice of £1,958 before the discount.	✓
Henderson & Co have duplicated an invoice in their system for £96.90 plus 20% VAT.	
2 credit notes for £49.71 and £67.77 have been omitted by Henderson & Co.	✓
The customer has paid for £117.48 of goods that they never received.	

Feedback: Item 1 – results in an underpayment of £1,958 × 6% = £117.48. Item 2 – the duplicated invoice amounts to a gross amount of £96.90 × 120% = £116.28. Item 3 – The credit notes amount to £117.48 resulting in a payment less than expected. Item 4 – If the customer paid for goods not received it would result in an overpayment.

PROCESS SUPPLIER TRANSACTIONS

35 NAN NURSING

(a) Has the correct purchase price of the chocolate puddings been charged on the invoice?   N

(b) Has the correct discount been applied?   Y

(c) What would be the VAT amount charged if the invoice was correct?   £18.00

(d) What would be the total amount charged if the invoice was correct?   £108.00

36 PIXIE PAPER

(a) Has the correct product been supplied by Pixie Paper?   Y

(b) Has the correct net price been calculated?   N

(c) Has the total invoice price been calculated correctly?   N

(d) What would be the VAT amount charged if the invoice was correct?   £90.00

(e) What would be the total amount charged if the invoice was correct?   £540.00

Feedback re (b) – the trade discount of 10% should have been deducted so that the net price was £450. VAT @ 20% on the net price of £450 is then calculated as £90.00.

37 PAINTS R US

(a) Has the correct product been supplied?   Y

(b) Has the correct net price been calculated?   Y

(c) Has the total invoice price been calculated correctly?   N

(d) What would be the VAT amount charged if the invoice was correct?   £32.00

(e) What would be the total amount charged if the invoice was correct?   £192.00

38 MT MOTORS

(a) B   £400.00

	£
List price	500
Less: Trade discount (20% × £500)	(100)
Purchases	400

(b) **B** £80.00

	£
List price	500.00
Less: Trade discount	(100.00)
Net purchases	400.00
VAT @ 20%	80.00
	480.00

(c) **A** It is issued to a supplier to request supply of goods from them on terms specified within the order.

39 ECHO LTD

(a)

Has the correct discount been applied?	N
How much should the trade discount amount be?	£100
What would be the VAT amount charged if the invoice was correct?	£180

(b)

Daybook: Purchase daybook					
Date 20XX	**Details**	**Invoice No:**	**Total £**	**VAT £**	**Net £**
10 Dec	Messi Brothers	**1365**	2,250	375	1,875

40 GORDON'S TRAIN REPAIRS

(a)

Daybook	✓
Sales daybook	
Purchases daybook	
Cashbook	
Purchase returns daybook	✓
Sales returns daybook	
Discounts allowed daybook	

(b)

Date 20XX	Supplier	Credit note number	Net £	VAT £	Total £
17 May	Narrow Gauge Ltd	CN869	317.60	63.52	381.12
26 June	Island of Sodor plc	CN0289	84.00	16.80	100.80
8 Aug	Topham Hatt & Co	421	98.50	19.70	118.20
13 Sep	Flying Kipper Ltd	C980	206.00	41.20	247.20
14 Oct	Gordon's Train Repairs	CN483	476.50	95.30	571.80
		Totals	1,182.60	236.52	1,419.12

(c)

Discrepancy	✓
Date of invoice	
Product type	
Quantity of product	
Unit price	✓
VAT rate	
Total	✓

Feedback: The total does not cast correctly.

41 NORMAN PRICE & CO

(a)

Daybook	✓
Sales daybook	
Purchases daybook	✓
Cashbook	
Purchase returns daybook	
Sales returns daybook	
Discounts allowed daybook	

(b)

Date 20XX	Supplier	Invoice number	Net £	VAT £	Total £
8 Mar	Norris Ltd	3897	1,010.00	202.00	1,212.00
10 Mar	Sam Jones	0187	878.40	175.68	1,054.08
11 Mar	James & Sarah Ltd	402929	463.80	92.76	556.56
11 Mar	Trevor Dylis Ltd	73910	1,329.10	265.82	1,594.92
14 Mar	Henry's Office Supplies	7208	584.00	116.80	700.80
		Totals	4,265.30	853.06	5,118.36

(c)

Discrepancy	✓
Prompt payment discount value	
VAT	✓
Invoice number	✓
Total	

Feedback: The VAT should be £2.70 calculated as £135 × 2% or £13.50 × 20%

42 FREDDIE LTD

Purchases daybook

Date 20XX	Details	Invoice number	Total £	VAT £	Net £	Product 14211 £	Product 14212 £
31 July	Box Ltd	2177	960	160	800	800	
31 July	Shrew Ltd	2175	14,400	2,400	12,000	12,000	
31 July	Novot & Co	2176	4,800	800	4,000		4,000
	Totals		20,160	3,360	16,800	12,800	4,000

43   **ALPHA LTD**

   (a)

Purchase return £900

   (b)

Invoice 486

   (c)

£8,580.00

44   **MAXIMUS LTD**

   (a)

<table>
<tr><td colspan="3" align="center">**Alpha Ltd**</td></tr>
<tr><td colspan="3" align="center">**121 Baker St**</td></tr>
<tr><td colspan="3" align="center">**Newcastle, NE1 7DJ**</td></tr>
<tr><td colspan="3" align="center">**REMITTANCE ADVICE**</td></tr>
<tr><td colspan="2">**To:** Maximus Ltd 20XX</td><td>**Date:** 31 Aug</td></tr>
<tr><td colspan="3">Please find attached our cheque in payment of the following amounts.</td></tr>
<tr><td align="center">**Invoice number**</td><td align="center">**Credit note number**</td><td align="center">**Amount**
£</td></tr>
<tr><td align="center">864</td><td></td><td align="center">6,386</td></tr>
<tr><td></td><td align="center">252</td><td align="center">964</td></tr>
<tr><td></td><td align="center">258</td><td align="center">1,218</td></tr>
<tr><td></td><td></td><td></td></tr>
<tr><td></td><td></td><td></td></tr>
<tr><td></td><td align="right">**Total amount paid**</td><td align="center">**4,204**</td></tr>
</table>

   (b)

   A remittance note is for our records only   F

   A remittance note is sent to a supplier to advise them of the amount being paid   T

45 HOLLY LTD

(a)

Purchase return 286

(b)

£928.80

(c)

£172.00

(d)

£1,032.00

46 EP MANUFACTURERS

(a)

Cheque for £1,200

(b)

Invoice 488

(c)

£4,850.00

47 STANNY LTD

(a)

Ringo Rings

37 Parker Lane

Stoke SK1 0KE

REMITTANCE ADVICE

To: Stanny Ltd **Date:** 31 Mar 20XX

Please find attached our cheque in payment of the following amounts.

Invoice number	Credit note number	Amount £
694		2,300
658		3,640
	198	650
	154	1,250
	Total amount paid	**4,040**

(b)

A remittance note is for our and the suppliers records   T

A remittance note is sent by a supplier confirming amounts received from them   F

48   TOYWORLD

(a)

Cheque for £500

Picklist: Invoice 207, Invoice 310, Invoice 504, Invoice 505, Cheque for £3,400, Cheque for £500

(b)

Invoice 505

Picklist: Invoice 207, Invoice 310, Invoice 504, Invoice 505, Cheque for £3,400, Cheque for £500

(c)

£4,000

49   HENRY HOUSE

(a)

<table>
<tr><td colspan="3" align="center">**Henry House**
22 Nursery Road
Keighley, BD22 7BD

REMITTANCE ADVICE</td></tr>
<tr><td colspan="3">**To:** Abbies Party
Date: 31 August 20XX
Please find attached our cheque in payment of the following amounts.</td></tr>
<tr><td>**Invoice number**</td><td>**Credit note number**</td><td>**Amount**
£</td></tr>
<tr><td align="center">242</td><td></td><td align="center">220</td></tr>
<tr><td></td><td align="center">27</td><td align="center">82</td></tr>
<tr><td></td><td></td><td></td></tr>
<tr><td></td><td></td><td></td></tr>
<tr><td colspan="2" align="right">**Total amount paid**</td><td align="center">138</td></tr>
</table>

(b)

D   The remittance advice note will be sent to the supplier to advise them of the amount being paid

50   GREY GARAGES

Remittance advice			
To: Mulberry Motors			
From: Grey Garages			
Payment method: BACS		**Date of payment:** 25 July	

Items outstanding			Tick if included in payment
Date 20XX	**Details**	**Amount** £	
23-Jun	Invoice 213	740	✓
06-Jul	Credit note 14	120	✓
13-Jul	Invoice 216	620	✓
19-Jul	Invoice 257	870	
	Total amount paid		£1,240

51   ERRICO

Supplier	£	Date by which the payment should be received by the supplier
Giacomo	67.51	11 June 20XX
Gaetani	39.33	9 June 20XX

52   LEWIN & CO

(a)

Supplier	£	Date by which the payment should be received by the supplier
Bridge Brothers	110.25	23rd October
Mitchells	128.79	24th October

(b)

Xcess Stock Unit 7 Windy Industrial Estate Irvine, KA6 8HU To: Lewin & Co Date: 31 Dec 20XX			Not to be paid
Date 20XX	Details	Transaction amount £	
12 Dec	Invoice 1001	1,700	
13 Dec	Invoice 1003	1,500	✓
21 Dec	Invoice 1004	2,350	
21 Dec	Credit note 101	940	
22 Dec	Invoice 1005	450	✓
27 Dec	Invoice 1010	470	
28 Dec	Credit note 102	50	✓

(c)

£3,580

(d)

£1,516

53 ASHBOURNE LTD

(a)

Supplier name	Invoice amount £	Invoice date 20XX	Amount to be paid £	Date by which supplier should receive payment
Kennack & Co	756.90	9 Jan	756.90	8 February
Butterworth & Sons	1,317.83	11 Jan	1,317.83	10 February
Jermyn Ltd	847.60	10 Jan	805.22	17 January

Feedback: Only Jermyn Ltd should be paid early as the others do not offer discounts of 5% or more. The payment will be £847.60 × 95% = £805.22

(b)

Transactions	✓
Opening balance	✓
Invoice 287	✓
Invoice 294	
Invoice 304	✓
Invoice 307	
Invoice 307	
Credit note 045	
Invoice 342	

Feedback: The payment of £5,296 = £639 + £1,204 + £3,453.

(c)

Type of error	✓
Underpayment	
Overpayment	
Missing transactions	
Duplicate transaction	✓
Timing difference	

Feedback: Invoice 307 is recorded twice.

54 FARFIELD LTD

(a)

Supplier name	Invoice amount £	Invoice date 20XX	Amount to be paid £	Date by which supplier should receive payment
Archer Joinery	1,340.00	25 Aug	1,340.00	31 August
Sankey Electrical	4,372.80	26 Aug	4,263.48	9 September
Pannal Construction	3,720.00	26 Aug	3,608.40	5 September

(b)

Transactions	✓
Opening balance	✓
Invoice 308	
Invoice 314	✓
Credit note 048	✓
Invoice 326	
Invoice 338	
Invoice 343	

Feedback: the cheque for £1,605 = £1,160 + £1,342 – £897

(c)

Type of error	✓
Underpayment	
Timing difference	✓
Overpayment	
Missing transactions	
Duplicate transaction	

Feedback: The difference of £896 relates to CHQ 0786 which was presumably sent by Farfield Ltd before the month end but received by Kelham builders on 2 October.

PROCESS RECEIPTS AND PAYMENTS

55   ABC LTD

(a)   Cash book – Credit side

Details	Cash	Bank	VAT	Payables	Cash purchases	Repairs and renewals
Balance b/f						
S. Lampard	216		36		180	
S. Bobbins	264		44		220	
Penny Rhodes	530				530	
Henley's Ltd		4,925		4,925		
Epic Equipment Maintenance		480	80			400
Total	**1,010**	**5,405**	**160**	**4,925**	**930**	**400**

(b) Cash book – Debit side

Details	Cash	Bank	Receivables
Balance b/f	1,550	7,425	
D Davies		851	851
E Denholm		450	450
Total	**1,550**	**8,726**	**1,301**

(c) Using your answers to (a) and (b) above calculate the cash balance.

£540

(d) Using your answers to (a) and (b) above calculate the bank balance.

£3,321

(e) Debit

56   BEDS

(a)   Cash book – Credit side

Details	Cash	Bank	VAT	Payables	Cash purchases	Repairs and renewals
Balance b/f						
A. Blighty Ltd	708		118		590	
R Bromby	228		38		190	
Roxy Bland	230				230	
Burgess Ltd		2,400		2,400		
Fast Equipment Repairs		96	16			80
Total	**1,166**	**2,496**	**172**	**2,400**	**1,010**	**80**

(b)   Cash book – Debit side

Details	Cash	Bank	Receivables
Balance b/f	1,175	3,825	
A Barnett		698	698
H Connelly		250	250
Total	**1,175**	**4,773**	**948**

(c) Using your answers to (a) and (b) above calculate the cash balance.

£9

(d) Using your answers to (a) and (b) above calculate the bank balance.

£2,277

(e) Will the bank balance calculated in (d) above be a debit or credit balance?

Debit

57   JO'S

(a)   **Cash book – credit side**

Details	Cash	Bank	VAT	Payables	Cash purchases	Stationery expenses
Bal b/f		19,546				
T. Hunkin Ltd	48		8		40	
Victoria Green	96		16		80	
B. Head Ltd	455				455	
Smiths Ltd		4,250		4,250		
Arrow Valley Stationers		120	20			100
Total	599	23,916	44	4,250	575	100

(b)   **Cash book – debit side**

Details	Cash	Bank	Receivables
Balance b/f	986		
J Drummond		623	623
N Atkinson		425	425
Total	986	1,048	1,048

(c)   **Using your answers to (a) and (b) above calculate the cash balance.**

£387

(d)   **Using your answers to (a) and (b) above calculate the bank balance.**

£22,868

(e)   **Will the bank balance calculated in (d) above be a debit or a credit balance?**

Credit

58   CARTER

(a)   **Cash book – Credit side**

Details	Cash	Bank	VAT	Payables	Cash purchases	Motor expenses
Balance b/f		11,450				
J Pumpkin	960		160		800	
B Row	240		40		200	
Lemon Ltd		100		100		
Remo Motor		240	40			200
Fencer		600		600		
Total	1,200	12,390	240	700	1,000	200

(b)   **Cash book – Debit side**

Details	Cash	Bank	Receivables
Balance b/f	1,850		
Jeff Jolly		127	127
Dolly Darton		310	310
Total	1,850	437	437

(c)

£650

(d)

£11,953

(e)

Credit

59   MANGROVE

Date 20XX	Details	Cash £	Bank £	VAT £	Cash purchases	Payables £
25 May	K Quick	334.80		55.80	279.00	
26 May	Whiles Ltd		1,374.00			1,374.00
27 May	Sasha and Co	418.80		69.80	349.00	

Feedback: K Quick VAT = £279.00 × 20% = £55.80. No VAT is recorded for Whiles Ltd as this payment settles a trade payable. The VAT would have been recorded when the original invoice was recorded in the purchases daybook. Sasha and Co VAT = £418.80 × 20/120 = £69.80.

60   SWAMP

(a)

Date 20XX	Details	Cash £	Bank £	VAT £	Cash sales	Receiv-ables
23 Aug	Bal b/f	1,089.70	8,539.43			
23 Aug	Bennett Ltd		2,924.40			2,924.40
25 Aug	J Smith	586.56		97.76	488.80	
		1,676.26	11,463.83			

(b)

£	862.78

Feedback: No VAT is shown relating to the credit customer as it is dealt with in the sales daybook. The credit side of the cash book shows the total cash payments were £813.48.

61 QUEEN VIC

(a)

Amount in petty cash box	**£141.00**
Balance on petty cash account	**£145.00**
Difference	**£4.00**

(b)

Petty cash reimbursement	
Date: 31.07.20XX	
Amount required to restore the cash in the petty cash box.	**£122.75**

62 THE ARCHES

(a) – (b)

Petty cash book

Debit side		Credit side					
Details	Amount £	Details	Amount £	VAT £	Postage £	Travel £	Stationery £
Balance b/f	200.00	Mick's Motors	20.00			20.00	
		Stamps	19.00		19.00		
		Office Essentials	26.40	4.40			22.00
		Balance c/d	134.60				
	200.00		**200.00**	**4.40**	**19.00**	**20.00**	**22.00**

63 RAINBOW

(a) – (b)

Petty cash book

Debit side		Credit side					
Details	Amount £	Details	Amount £	VAT £	Postage £	Travel £	Stationery £
Balance b/f	100.00	Colin's Cabs	28.00			28.00	
		Post Office	18.00		18.00		
		ABC Stationery	38.40	6.40			32.00
		Balance c/d	15.60				
	100.00		**100.00**	**6.40**	**18.00**	**28.00**	**32.00**

64   SOOTY & SWEEP

(a)

Amount in petty cash box	£127.40
Balance on petty cash account	£135.00
Difference	£7.60

(b)

Petty cash reimbursement	
Date: 31.07.20XX	
Amount required to restore the cash in the petty cash box.	£245.00

65   JAWS DENTISTRY

(a) – (b)

Petty cash book

Debit side		Credit side					
Details	Amount £	Details	Amount £	VAT £	Postage £	Travel £	Stationery £
Balance b/f	225.00	Ace Taxis	26.00			26.00	
		Kate's Couriers	27.00		27.00		
		Smiths Stationery	45.60	7.60			38.00
		Balance c/d	126.40				
	225.00		225.00	7.60	27.00	26.00	38.00

66   TOM'S TILES

(a)

Amount in petty cash box	**£162.12**
Balance on petty cash account	**£165.52**
Difference	**£3.40**

(b)

Petty cash reimbursement	
Date: 30.04.20XX	
Amount required to restore the cash in the petty cash box.	**£224.12**

67   ROCKY RILEY

(a) – (b)

Petty cash book

Debit side		Credit side					
Details	Amount £	Details	Amount £	VAT £	Postage £	Travel £	Stationery £
Balance b/f	175.00	Kath's Kars	32.00			32.00	
		Stamps	25.00		25.00		
		Pauline's Pens	24.00	4.00			20.00
		Balance c/d	94.00				
	175.00		175.00	**4.00**	**25.00**	**32.00**	**20.00**

68   MHAIRI MOTORS

(a)

Amount in petty cash box	**£99.80**
Balance on petty cash account	**£110.00**
Difference	**£10.20**

(b)

Petty cash reimbursement	
Date: 31.07.20XX	
Amount required to restore the cash in the petty cash box.	**£191.50**

69 DAINTY DESIGNS

(a)

VAT £	Net £
5.20	26.00

(b)

£91.66

(c)

Details	Amount £	Debit ✓	Credit ✓
Cash from bank	237.70	✓	

(d)

Details	Amount £	Debit ✓	Credit ✓
Balance c/d	280.00		✓

(e)

Petty cash voucher	Total £	VAT £	Net £
222	32.40	5.40	27.00
223	12.00	2.00	10.00

70 JACKSON MOTORING

(a)

VAT £	Net £
3.60	18.00

(b)

£33.50

(c)

Details	Amount £	Debit ✓	Credit ✓
Cash from bank	183.45	✓	

(d)

Details	Amount £	Debit ✓	Credit ✓
Balance c/d	215.00		✓

(e)

Petty cash voucher	Total £	VAT £	Net £
120	20.00	0	20.00
121	19.20	3.20	16.00

71 WHILES LTD

(a)

Details	Amount £	Debit ✓	Credit ✓
See below	302.17	✓	

Details	✓
Balance brought down	
Bank	✓
Sales	
Cash	

Feedback: In an imprest system the amounts paid from petty cash are then transferred from the bank account in order to maintain the float.

(b)

	✓
A missing petty cash voucher for £16.67 excluding VAT	✓
Cash of £20 has been stolen from petty cash	
A petty cash voucher for £20 has yet to be recorded in the petty cash book	
A petty cash transaction of £64.20 was incorrectly recorded in the petty cash book as £84.20	✓

Feedback: The missing petty cash voucher would be £16.67 × 120% = £20 which is the difference between the vouchers and petty cash book totals. Stolen cash would not affect the vouchers recording expenditure or the petty cash book itself. If the petty cash voucher had not been recorded then the vouchers would exceed the petty cash book total. This error of £20 results in the petty cash book expenditure exceeding the amount of the vouchers.

(c)

£	64.00

Feedback: The VAT would be recognised separately in the VAT column of the petty cash book. The net expenditure on cleaning is (£48 × 100/120) + £24 = £64.

72   BAKER LTD

Date 20XX	Details	Cash £	VAT £	Cleaning £	Travel £	Food/drink £	Stationery £
30 Nov	Bal b/f	89.40	14.90	14.50	36.00	–	12.00
30 Nov	Window cleaning	28.50	4.75	23.75			
30 Nov	A4 binders	43.20	7.20				36.00

73   BUTCHER LTD

(a)   **Set up the recurring entry in the digital bookkeeping system**

Transaction type	General ledger code	Start date 20XX	End date 20XX	Frequency	Net amount £	VAT code
Bank	Option 1	Option 2	Option 3	Monthly	25.00	Option 4

Option 1	✓
7100 – Insurance	
1100 – Van non-current assets	
2000 – Bank	
7400 – Motor lease costs	✓

Option 2	✓
5 Jun 20XX	
5 May 20XX	✓
5 Nov 20XX	
5 Dec 20XX	

Option 3	✓
5 Jun 20XX	
5 May 20XX	
5 Nov 20XX	
5 Dec 20XX	✓

Option 4	✓
V0 – 0%	
V1 – Exempt	
V20 – 20%	✓
V5 – 5%	

(b)   **Identify ONE effect of processing the recurring entry.**

Effect	✓
The standing order will be automatically set up to pay for the lease costs	
Entries will be posted to all relevant general ledger accounts	✓
Entries will be posted to the receivables ledger and all relevant general ledger accounts	

74 CHANDLER LTD

(a)

Information	✓
The number of recurring transactions	
The frequency of the recurring transactions	
The total value of all recurring transactions	✓
The VAT rate	

(b)

Transaction type	General ledger code	Start date 20XX	End date 20XX	Frequency	Net amount £	VAT code
Bank	Option 1	Option 2	Option 3	Monthly	400	Option 4

Option 1	✓
7560 – Rent expense	
1040 – Office equipment	
2000 – Bank	
4000 – Maintenance services	✓

Option 2	✓
10 Apr 20XX	
10 May 20XX	
10 Feb 20XX	✓
10 Jul 20XX	

Option 3	✓
10 Apr 20XX	
10 May 20XX	
10 Feb 20XX	
10 Jul 20XX	✓

Option 4	✓
V0 – 0%	
V1 – Exempt	
V20 – 20%	✓
V5 – 5%	

PROCESS TRANSACTIONS INTO LEDGER ACCOUNTS

75   LADY LTD

General ledger

Payables ledger control account

	£		£
		1 Dec Balance b/d	5,103.90
		18 Dec Purchases & Vat	**903.23**

VAT account

	£		£
		1 Dec Balance b/d	526.90
18 Dec PLCA	**150.53**		

Purchases account

	£		£
1 Dec Balance b/d	22,379.52		
18 Dec PLCA	**752.70**		

Subsidiary ledger

M Brown

	£		£
		1 Dec Balance b/d	68.50
		1 Dec PDB	**300.00**

H Madden

	£		£
		1 Dec Balance b/d	286.97
		5 Dec PDB	**183.55**

L Singh

	£		£
		1 Dec Balance b/d	125.89
		7 Dec PDB	**132.60**

A Stevens

	£		£
		1 Dec Balance b/d	12.36
		10 Dec PDB	**90.00**

N Shema

	£		£
		1 Dec Balance b/d	168.70
		18 Dec PDB	**197.08**

76 BUTTONS LTD

(a)

Account name	Amount £	Debit ✔	Credit ✔
Peak & Co	6,240		✔
Max Ltd	12,720		✔
McIntyre Wholesale	5,760		✔
Pigmy Ltd	3,744		✔

(b)

Account name	Amount £	Debit ✔	Credit ✔
Purchases	23,720	✔	
VAT	4,744	✔	
Payables ledger control	28,464		✔

77 SPARKY LTD

(a) **Receivables ledger**

Account name	Amount £	Debit ✔	Credit ✔
Clarkson Ltd	1,680		✔
Kyle & Co	720		✔

(b)   General ledger

Account name	Amount £	Debit ✓	Credit ✓
Receivables ledger control account	2,400		✓
Sales returns	2,000	✓	
VAT	400	✓	

78   LOUIS LTD

(a)

Account name	Amount £	Debit ✓	Credit ✓
Sheep & Co	3,840	✓	
Cow Ltd	11,760	✓	
Chicken & Partners	6,720	✓	
Pig Ltd	14,496	✓	

(b)

Account name	Amount £	Debit ✓	Credit ✓
Receivables ledger control	36,816	✓	
VAT	6,136		✓
Sales	30,680		✓

79   THOMAS & TILLY

(a)   Payables ledger

Account name	Amount £	Debit ✓	Credit ✓
May Ltd	1,920	✓	
Hammond & Co	1,200	✓	

(b)   General ledger

Account name	Amount £	Debit ✓	Credit ✓
Payables ledger control account	3,120	✓	
Purchase returns	2,600		✓
VAT	520		✓

80 FINCH'S

(a)

Account name	Amount £	Debit ✓	Credit ✓
Lou and Phil's	5,040	✓	
Eddie and Co	10,560	✓	
Noah's Arc	2,880	✓	
Alex and Freddie	720	✓	

(b)

Account name	Amount £	Debit ✓	Credit ✓
Sales	16,000		✓
VAT	3,200		✓
Receivables ledger control	19,200	✓	

81 JESSICA & CO

(a) **Payables ledger**

Account name	Amount £	Debit ✓	Credit ✓
Iona Ltd	1,680	✓	
Matilda Ltd	4,320	✓	

(b) **General ledger**

Account name	Amount £	Debit ✓	Credit ✓
Payables ledger control account	6,000	✓	
Purchases returns	5,000		✓
VAT	1,000		✓

82   HORSEY REACH

(a)

Account name	Amount £	Debit ✓	Credit ✓
Receivables ledger control	226.80		✓
VAT	37.80	✓	
Discounts allowed	189.00	✓	

(b)

Account name	Amount £	Debit ✓	Credit ✓
Ashleigh Buildings	36.00		✓
143 WGT	54.00		✓
McDuff McGregor	43.20		✓
Cameron Travel	93.60		✓

83   BUTTERFLY BEES

(a)

Account name	Amount £	Debit ✓	Credit ✓
Discounts received	356.00		✓
VAT	71.20		✓
Payables ledger control	427.20	✓	

(b)

Account name	Amount £	Debit ✓	Credit ✓
Bella Bumps	24.00	✓	

84   OLIVIA ROSE BRIDAL SUPPLIES

(a)

Account name	Amount £	Debit ✓	Credit ✓
Discounts allowed	189.00	✓	
VAT	37.80	✓	
Receivables ledger control	226.80		✓

(b)

Account name	Amount £	Debit ✓	Credit ✓
Bridezilla	54.00		✓

85   SUSSEX TRADING

(a)

Account name	Amount £	Debit ✓	Credit ✓
Discounts allowed	410.00	✓	
VAT	82.00	✓	
Receivables ledger control	492.00		✓

(b)

Account name	Amount £	Debit ✓	Credit ✓
Woody Woodburn	78.00		✓

86   ROXY CAKE DESIGNS

(a)

Account name	Amount £	Debit ✓	Credit ✓
Discounts allowed	318.00	✓	
VAT	63.60	✓	
Receivables ledger control	381.60		✓

(b)

Account name	Amount £	Debit ✓	Credit ✓
Percy Tran	33.60		✓

87 ANNANDALE SUPPLIES

(a)

Account name	Amount £	Debit/Credit
Purchases returns	4,580.00	Credit
VAT	916.00	Credit
Payables ledger control	5,496.00	Debit

(b)

Account name	Amount £	Debit/Credit
Sales returns	2,501.00	Debit
VAT	500.20	Debit
Receivables ledger control	3,001.20	Credit

88 NC CLEANING SUPPLIES

(a)

Account name	Amount £	Debit/Credit
Payables ledger control	318.00	Debit
VAT	53.00	Credit
Purchases returns	265.00	Credit

(b)

Account name	Amount £	Debit/Credit
Sales returns	150.00	Debit
VAT	30.00	Debit
Receivables ledger control	180.00	Credit

89   CHUGGER LTD

(a)   **General ledger**

Account name	Amount £	Debit ✓	Credit ✓
Stationery expense	80	✓	
Repairs	200	✓	
VAT	56	✓	

(b)   **Receivables ledger**

Account name	Amount £	Debit ✓	Credit ✓
BBG Ltd	7,200		✓
EFG Ltd	5,000		✓

(c)   **General ledger**

Account name	Amount £	Debit ✓	Credit ✓
Receivables ledger control	12,200		✓

90   ITALIAN STALLIONS

(a)   **General ledger**

Account name	Amount £	Debit ✓	Credit ✓
Office supplies	80	✓	
Repairs	160	✓	
VAT	48	✓	

(b)   **Receivables ledger**

Account name	Amount £	Debit ✓	Credit ✓
AAG Ltd	4,000		✓
HLG Ltd	3,000		✓

(c)   **General ledger**

Account name	Amount £	Debit ✓	Credit ✓
Receivables ledger control	7,000		✓

91   FRED'S FISH

(a)   **Receivables ledger**

Account name	Amount £	Debit ✓	Credit ✓
K and D Ltd	8,200		✓

(b)   **General ledger**

Account name	Amount £	Debit ✓	Credit ✓
Receivables ledger control	8,200		✓

(c)   **General ledger**

Account name	Amount £	Debit ✓	Credit ✓
Stationery	100	✓	
VAT	20	✓	
Postage	800	✓	

92   HICKORY HOUSE

General ledger

Account name	Amount £	Debit ✓	Credit ✓
VAT	6.80	✓	
Postage	15.00	✓	
Motor expenses	12.40	✓	
Office expenses	21.60	✓	
Bank	90		✓

93   MESSI & CO

General ledger

Account name	Amount £	Debit ✓	Credit ✓
VAT	7.25	✓	
Postage	4.50	✓	
Motor expenses	8.00	✓	
Office expenses	28.28	✓	
Petty cash control	48.03		✓

94 STAVROS

General ledger

Account name	Amount £	Debit ✓	Credit ✓
VAT	18.86	✓	
Postage	16.00	✓	
Business travel	30.80	✓	
Sundry expenses	63.50	✓	
Bank	110.00		✓

95 YUMMY CUPCAKES

General ledger

Account name	Amount £	Debit ✓	Credit ✓
VAT	11.07	✓	
Sundry expenses	10.00	✓	
Business travel	45.37	✓	
Postage	4.00	✓	
Petty cash control	70.44		✓

96 OOH LA!

General ledger

Account name	Amount £	Debit ✓	Credit ✓
VAT	15.21	✓	
Postage	36.30	✓	
Sundry expenses	35.05	✓	
Motor expenses	17.00	✓	
Bank	70.00		✓

97 LJ INTERIORS

Account name	Amount £	Debit ✓	Credit ✓
VAT	64.00	✓	
Stationery	320.00	✓	
Postage	32.00	✓	
Charitable donations	150.00	✓	

98   KAZ KARATE CLUB

Account name	Amount £	Debit ✔	Credit ✔
VAT	31.00	✔	
Motor expenses	155.00	✔	
Postage	20.00	✔	
Insurance	180.00	✔	

99   JACINTA INTERIOR DESIGN

(a)

Petty cash reimbursement	
Week 22	
Amount required to restore the cash in the petty cash box.	**£243.90**

	£
Stationery	42.30
Travelling cost	76.50
Refreshments	38.70
Sundry payables (£72.00 × (120/100)	86.40
	243.90 to restore to £300

(b)

A   Dr Petty cash   Cr Bank

100   MARTHA

(a)

VAT £	Net £
10.00	50.00

(b)

£62.40

(c)

Details	Amount £	Debit ✔	Credit ✔
Cash from bank	117.36	✔	

(d)

Details	Amount £	Debit ✓	Credit ✓
Balance c/d	150.00		✓

(e)

Petty cash receipt	Analysis column	Amount £
Newark Printers	Office expenses	14.50
ERJ Motor Supplies	Motor expenses	32.00
Co-pop	Cleaning expenses	5.00

101 ROLAND

(a)

Account name	Amount £	Debit ✓	Credit ✓
Receivables ledger control	123.60		✓
VAT	20.60	✓	
Discounts allowed	103.00	✓	

(b)

Account name	Amount £	Debit ✓	Credit ✓
Aldo & Co	24.00		✓
Hopley Brothers	36.00		✓
Fernando's	25.20		✓
Richmond Travel	38.40		✓

102 ROGER

(a)   Receivables ledger

Account name	Amount £	Debit ✓	Credit ✓
TUV Ltd	4,000		✓

(b)   General ledger

Account name	Amount £	Debit ✓	Credit ✓
Receivables ledger control	4,000		✓

(c)   **General ledger**

Account name	Amount £	Debit ✓	Credit ✓
Entertainment	160	✓	
VAT	32	✓	
Insurance	240	✓	

103   ANDREW, WILLIAM & CO

(a)

Account name	Amount £	Debit ✓	Credit ✓
Cash purchases	4,345.70	✓	
VAT	869.14	✓	
Payables ledger control account	8,671.46	✓	

Feedback: The full journal is

Dr Input VAT   £869.14

Dr Purchases £4,345.70

Dr Payables £8,671.46

Cr Cash £3,574.70

Cr Bank £10,311.60

(b)

Daybook	Debit ✓	Credit ✓	Payables ledger ✓	Receivables ledger ✓
Purchases		✓	✓	
Discounts allowed		✓		✓

Feedback: Credit purchases (from the purchases daybook) are credited to payables. Discounts allowed are given to customers and reduce (credit) the receivables balance

104 S WILLIAMS LTD

(a)

Account name	Amount £	Debit ✓	Credit ✓
Cash sales	2,045.60		✓
VAT	2,013.10		✓
Receivables ledger control account	8,019.90		✓

(b)

Daybook	Debit ✓	Credit ✓	Payables ledger ✓	Receivables ledger ✓
Sales		✓		✓
Discounts received	✓		✓	

Feedback: The sales day book records credit sales so the entries affect the receivables ledger. Discounts received come from suppliers reducing our trade payables balance.

105 BROOKLYN BOATS

(a) – (c)

Electricity

Date 20XX	Details	Amount £	Date 20XX	Details	Amount £
01 Dec	Balance b/f	870	31 Dec	Balance c/d	1,220
12 Dec	Bank	350			
	Total	1,220		**Total**	1,220
		1,220			

Discounts received

Date 20XX	Details	Amount £	Date 20XX	Details	Amount £
31 Dec	Balance c/d	600	1 Dec	Balance b/f	500
			15 Dec	Payables Ledger control	100
	Total	600		**Total**	600
			1 Jan	Balance b/d	600

106   WIGGLE POGGLE LTD

(a) – (c)

Discount allowed

Date 20XX	Details	Amount £	Date 20XX	Details	Amount £
01 July	Balance b/f	1,560	31 July	Balance c/d	2,160
14 July	Receivables ledger control account	480			
16 July	Receivables ledger control account	120			
	Total	2,160		**Total**	2,160
1 Aug	Balance b/d	2,160			

Interest income

Date 20XX	Details	Amount £	Date 20XX	Details	Amount £
31 July	Balance c/d	400	01 July	Balance b/f	320
			28 July	Bank	80
	Total	400		**Total**	400
			1 Aug	Balance b/d	400

107   CRAZY CURTAINS

(a) – (c)

Electricity expense

Date 20XX	Details	Amount £	Date 20XX	Details	Amount £
01 Jan	Bal b/f	200	31 Jan	Balance c/d	450
22 Jan	Bank	250			
	Total	450		**Total**	450
1 Feb	Balance b/d	450			

Rental income

Date 20XX	Details	Amount £	Date 20XX	Details	Amount £
31 Jan	Balance c/d	1,000	01 Jan	Balance b/f	400
			28 Jan	Bank	600
	Total	1,000		**Total**	1,000
			1 Feb	Balance b/d	1,000

108 BALANCES 1

Account name	Balance c/d at 31 December £	Debit/Credit	Total shown in both the debit and credit columns £
Capital	6,000	Debit	6,000
Fixtures and Fittings	19,800	Credit	21,000
Loan	23,230	Debit	24,880
Drawings	2,450	Credit	2,450

109 BALANCES 2

Account name	Balance c/d at 31 March £	Debit/Credit	Total shown in both the debit and credit columns £
Capital	15,000	Debit	15,000
Plant and Machinery	8,950	Credit	9,750
Loan	14,180	Debit	15,200
Drawings	4,220	Credit	4,220

110 BALANCES 3

(a)

Account	Amount £	Debit ✓	Credit ✓
AD014	1,505		✓
AD019	3,174	✓	
AD036	21		✓

Feedback:

AD014

Date 20XX	Details	Amount £	Date 20XX	Details	Amount £
21 Dec	Bank	465	14 Dec	Cash	947
28 Dec	Bank	1,987			
				Bal c/d	1,505
		2,452			2,452

AD019

Date 20XX	Details	Amount £	Date 20XX	Details	Amount £
19 Dec	Cash	136	3 Dec	Bank	948
			12 Dec	Cash	2,362
	Bal c/d	3,174			
		3,310			3,310

AD036

Date 20XX	Details	Amount £	Date 20XX	Details	Amount £
7 Dec	Cash	754	3 Dec	Bank	856
18 Dec	Bank	429	27 Dec	Cash	306
				Bal c/d	21
		1,183			1,183

(b) **Receivables**

Date	Details	Amount £	Date	Details	Amount £
1 Dec	Balance brought down	9,864	17 Dec	Cash	7,493
21 Dec	Sales	4,928	31 Dec	Balance carried down	7,299
		14,792		Total	14,792
1 Jan	Balance brought down	7,299			

Section 3

MOCK ASSESSMENT QUESTIONS

You have **1 hour and 30 minutes** to complete this practice assessment.

This assessment contains **11 tasks** and you should attempt to complete **every** task,

- Each task is independent. You will not need to refer to your answers to previous tasks.

- The total number of marks for this assessment is 100.

- Read every task carefully to make sure you understand what is required.

- Where the date is relevant, it is given in the task data.

- Both minus signs and brackets can be used to indicate negative numbers **unless** task instructions state otherwise.

- You must use a full stop to indicate a decimal point. For example, write 100.57 **not** 100,57 or 10057.

- You may use a comma to indicate a number in the thousands, but you don't have to. For example, 10000 and 10,000 are both acceptable.

- Mathematical rounding should be applied where appropriate.

Scenario

- The tasks in this assessment are set in different business situations where the following apply:

- Businesses use a variety of bookkeeping systems.

- Double entry takes place in the general ledger.

- The VAT rate is 20%.

TASK 1 (10 MARKS)

This task is about manual and digital bookkeeping systems.

(a)   **Which document or report would be used for each of the purposes below?**

	Document or report
To identify which specific invoices are being paid off when sending payment	
To issue a refund or to write off an amount owed following a return of goods	
To show the detail of the goods sold and total price	
To show details of the amounts owed from each customer	

Picklist: Credit note, remittance, receivables ledger, sales invoice

(4 marks)

Product codes for specific toys sold consist of a sequentially numbered system based on the name of the product, sorted alphabetically. This is followed by the first two letters of the product type. The first three products in the warehouse are shown below, with the first one filled in.

(b)   **Identify the correct product codes for the items below.**

Product	Product Code
Aeroplane	01AE
Astronaut	
Alphabet Blocks	

(2 marks)

(c)   **Identify whether the following statements regarding manual bookkeeping systems are true or false.**

	True	False
The sales returns daybook is one of the books of prime entry		
A manual bookkeeping system can decrease the risk of errors when moving data from the books of prime entry to the ledgers		

(2 marks)

(d)   **Identify whether the following statements regarding digital bookkeeping systems are true or false.**

	True	False
A digital bookkeeping system automatically reconciles receivables and payables ledgers to the control accounts		
A digital bookkeeping system automatically balances the cash book		

(2 marks)

TASK 2 (10 MARKS)

This task is about principles of double-entry bookkeeping.

(a) **Identify the classification of each account.**

Account	Classification
Trade payable	
Computer equipment	
Discounts received	

Picklist: Asset, Liability, Income, Expense, Capital

(3 marks)

Pontoon Co has a total capital balance of £16,540 and total liabilities of £34,500.

(b) **Calculate the value of assets in Pontoon Co.**

£

(1 mark)

(c) **Identify the dual effect of each transaction by matching the dual effect from the picklist to the transaction identified. You should ignore VAT in this task.**

Transaction	Dual effect
A sale of goods on credit	
Received a new loan from the bank	
Payment to a credit supplier using the bank	
A purchase of a motor vehicle for cash	
Payment of fuel expenses for cash	
Receipt of cash from the owner	

Picklist
Increase in assets and capital
Increase in assets and income
Increase in expenses, decrease in assets
Increase in assets and liabilities
Both increase and decrease an asset
Decrease in assets and liabilities

(6 marks)

TASK 3 (10 MARKS)

This task is about processing customer invoices or credit notes and entering in daybooks.

A sales invoice is being prepared from the delivery note below.

Jeff's Jackets
Delivery note no. 4021
01 Dec 20X2
Customer account code: JJ01
500 cases of product A, product code 03FE

The list price of the goods was £40 per case plus VAT. Jeff's Jackets are to be given a 10% trade discount.

(a) Calculate the amounts to be included in the invoice.

	£
Amount before discount	
Discount given	
Amount after discount	
VAT	
Total	

(5 marks)

(b) Which daybook will the above transaction be entered in?

	£
Sales daybook	
Sales returns daybook	
Cash book	
Discounts allowed daybook	

(1 mark)

(c) Complete the daybook entry below

Date 20X2	Customer code	Invoice No:	Total £	VAT £	Net £
1 Dec		142			

(4 marks)

TASK 4 (10 MARKS)

This task is about processing receipts from customers.

Pontoon Co has received a cheque for £223 for the settlement of two invoices below. In addition to the two invoices, Pontoon Co had also given Buckley Co a credit note for £25 for faulty goods it had previously supplied.

Pontoon Co	
Invoice number 193	
To: Buckley Co 19 October 20X2	
	£
10 units product XJ45 @ £12 each	120.00
VAT @ 20%	24.00
Total	144.00

Pontoon Co	
Invoice number 194	
To: Buckley Co 20 October 20X2	
	£
5 units product XJ44 @ £9 each	45.00
VAT @ 20%	9.00
Total	54.00

(a)   **Complete the following statement:**

Buckley Co has _____GAP 1_____ so _____GAP 2_____.

Gap 1	✔
Overpaid Pontoon Co	
Underpaid Pontoon Co	
Paid Pontoon Co the correct amount	

Gap 2	✔
A refund is due	
A request for further payment should be made	
No further action is required	

(2 marks)

Pontoon Co has also received a cheque for £483 for the settlement of two invoices below. The cheque was received on 1 December 20X2. Pontoon Co offers Moran Co a 5% prompt payment if the payment is made within 20 days of the invoice date.

Pontoon Co	
Invoice number 213	
To: Moran Co 22 October 20X2	
	£
20 units product XJ45 @ £12 each	240.00
VAT @ 20%	48.00
Total	288.00

Pontoon Co	
Invoice number 219	
To: Moran Co 23 October 20X2	
	£
20 units product XJ44 @ £9 each	180.00
VAT @ 20%	36.00
Total	216.00

(b)   **Complete the following statement:**

Moran Co has _____GAP 1_____ so _____GAP 2_____.

Gap 1	✓
Overpaid Pontoon Co	
Underpaid Pontoon Co	
Paid Pontoon Co the correct amount	

Gap 2	✓
A refund is due	
A request for further payment should be made	
No further action is required	

(2 marks)

```
                    Pontoon Co
              Invoice number 253
To: Moran Co   25 November 20X2

                                    £

20 units product XJ23 @ £30 each    600.00
VAT @ 20%                           125.00
                                  _____
Total                              725.00
```

(c)   **If Moran Co pays the above invoice within 10 days and receives the prompt payment discount, what is the amount that Moran Co will pay?**

£ _____

(1 mark)

(d)   **How would Pontoon Co categorise the discount taken by Moran Co?**

	✓
Income	
Expense	
Asset	
Liability	

(1 mark)

Pontoon Co issued the following invoice to Leighton Co:

```
                    Pontoon Co
              Invoice number 268
To: Leighton Co   30 October 20X2

                                    £

15 units product XJ45 @ £12 each    180.00
Bulk discount 10%                   (18.00)
Net amount                          162.00
VAT @ 20%                            36.00
                                  _____
Total                              126.00
```

(e)   **Which TWO errors have Pontoon Co made in the above invoice?**

	✓
The total product cost is incorrectly calculated	
The bulk discount should not be applied until Pontoon Co know if the payment will be made on time	
The VAT figure is incorrectly calculated	
The total invoice amount is incorrectly calculated	

(2 marks)

Pontoon Co received the following remittance advice from Croft Co.

Remittance advice 1 November 20X2	
Invoice	£
145	600.00
183	125.00
Total	725.00

Pontoon Co' receivables ledger shows the following in respect of Croft:

Date 20X2	Details	Invoice number	Total £	VAT £	Net £
3 Oct	Croft Co	145	600	500	100
8 Oct	Croft Co	183	150	25	125

(f)   **Identify if the invoices have been paid correctly or not**

	Paid correctly ✓	Not paid correctly ✓
Invoice 145		
Invoice 183		

(2 marks)

TASK 5 (10 MARKS)

This task is about processing supplier invoices or credit notes and entering in daybooks.

The following invoice has been received from the credit supplier Clanker Co for goods that were received on 10 December 20X2. The warehouse staff have confirmed that the goods were received correctly. Clanker Co has a supplier code which is CLA05.

Clanker Co, Invoice No. 1365	
To: Pontoon Co, 10 Dec 20X2	
60 units of product YT653 @ £46 each	£2,760.00
VAT	£552.00
Total	£3,312.00

(a)   **Enter the details into the missing sections in the daybook.**

Date 20X2	Supplier code	Invoice No:	Total £	VAT £	Net £
10 Dec		1365			

(4 marks)

(b)   **Which daybook would this be entered into?**

	✓
Supplier's daybook	
Purchases daybook	
Cash book	
Sales daybook	

(1 mark)

Pontoon Co discovered later that three of the units were damaged and contacted the supplier in order to receive a credit note. This was agreed by Clanker Co and the credit note was issued before the payment from Pontoon Co was due.

(c)   **Which TWO of these items represent the dual effect in Pontoon Co's records when the credit note is received?**

	✓
Liabilities will decrease	
Assets will increase	
Expenses will decrease	
Income will increase	

(2 marks)

The purchasing department in Pontoon Co have recently received another purchase invoice from Clanker Co. They have then compared it to the purchase order and have noted some discrepancies.

Purchase order PO682

To: Clanker Co, 18 Dec 20X2
Order details:

15 units of product YT653 @ £46 each

Terms: 30 days

Clanker Co

Invoice No. 1940

To: Pontoon Co
19 Dec 20X2

15 units of product YT653 @ £46 each	£690.00
VAT	£103.50
Total	£3,312.00

Payment will be due on 3 January 20X3

(d)   **Identify the THREE discrepancies between the purchase order and the purchase invoice**

	✓
Net amount	
VAT calculation	
Total amount	
Payment terms	
Product supplied	
Quantity supplied	
Unit price	

(3 marks)

TASK 6 (10 MARKS)

This task is about processing payments to suppliers.

The two invoices below were received on 3 January from credit suppliers of Pontoon Co who offer prompt payment discounts.

Invoices:

Groves Ltd	
Invoice number 6836	
To: Pontoon Co 3 January 20X3	
	£
250 product code H43 @ £4.80 each	1,200.00
VAT @ 20%	240.00
Total	1,440.00
Terms: 5% prompt payment discount if payment is received within 10 days of the invoice date.	

Moore Ltd	
Invoice number 578	
To: Pontoon Co 3 January 20X3	
	£
140 product code TR6 @ £6.50 each	910.00
VAT @ 20%	182.00
Total	1,092.00
Terms: 10% prompt payment discount if payment is received within 5 days of the invoice date.	

(a) **Calculate the amount to be paid to each supplier if the prompt payment discount is taken and when the payment needs to be made .**

Supplier	£	Date by which to make the payment
Groves Ltd		
Moore Ltd		

(4 marks)

Pontoon Co has received a query from Bloomer Ltd, one of its suppliers. A member of the payments team sent Bloomer Ltd one cheque for £14,630 but did not send a remittance with it, so you have been asked to identify what amounts the cheques are paying off. Bloomer have sent a statement below.

Bloomer Ltd Customer statement		
To: Pontoon Co		
Date 20X2	Details	Transaction amount £
12 Dec	Invoice 345	10,450
13 Dec	Invoice 346	3,210
21 Dec	Invoice 347	2,000
21 Dec	Credit note 101	1,030
22 Dec	Invoice 348	230
27 Dec	Invoice 349	820
28 Dec	Credit note 102	50

(b) Which FOUR items should now be removed from the Bloomer Ltd customer statement now that the payment has been made?

Details	✓
Invoice 345	
Invoice 346	
Invoice 347	
Credit note 101	
Invoice 348	
Invoice 349	

(4 marks)

(c) What will be the amount remaining as owed to Bloomer Ltd?

£

(1 mark)

(d) **Which of the following statements regarding remittance advices is correct?**

Details	✓
Remittances are sent to the inventory department to advise them inventory has been paid for	
Remittances are sent to the customer to advise them of the amount being paid	
Remittances are sent to the bank to confirm payment is to be made	
Remittances are sent to the supplier to advise them of the amount being paid	

(1 mark)

TASK 7 (8 MARKS)

This task is about processing transactions in the cash book.

One of the finance team went to the bank today and paid in two amounts, the details of which are as follows:

Receipts

Cheque 000642	Cash sales paid in
From Broomes Co, paying all outstanding invoices	Total £560
Total £7,200 inclusive of VAT at 20%	

The cash sales all related to items that were zero-rated for VAT purposes.

Update the extract from the receipts section of the cash book below

Details	General ledger code	Total £	VAT £	Net £
Broomes Co	Picklist			
Cash sales	Picklist			

General ledger code picklist: 3463 Trade Receivables, 7420 Trade Payables, 6200 Sales, 5600 Purchases

(8 marks)

TASK 8 (6 MARKS)

This task is about processing transactions in the petty cash book.

Pontoon Co maintains an analytical petty cash book. At the end of the month, one of the accounts team at Pontoon Co withdraw enough money from the bank to ensure the balance on petty cash is at £300.

Details of the transactions in the petty cash book for the last month are shown below.

Petty cash-book

Date 20X3	Details	Amount £	Date 20XX	Details	Amount £	VAT £	Office expenses £
			15 Jan	Team lunch	60.00	10.00	50.00
			17 Jan	Coffee & milk	15.00	2.50	12.50

(a) **What will be the entries required at 31 January to restore the total of the petty cash back up to £300?**

Details	Amount £	Debit ✓	Credit ✓

Details picklist: Amount, Balance b/d, Balance c/d, Cash from bank

(3 marks)

(b) **What is the entry made in the petty cash book to record the closing balance on 30 June?**

Details	Amount £	Debit ✓	Credit ✓

Details picklist: Amount, Balance b/d, Balance c/d, Cash from bank

(3 marks)

TASK 9 (6 MARKS)

This task is about processing recurring entries.

Today's date is 20 January 20X3. Your supervisor has asked you to set up a recurring payment for services for confidential waste disposal for a one-year fixed-term contract. The total amount is for £660 a year, payable in monthly instalments on the 28th day of each month.

(a)   Set up the recurring entry

Transaction type	Details	Start date	Frequency	End date	Amount £
Recurring payment					

Picklists:

Details	✓
640 – Bank	
7420 – Trade payables	
1560 – Office expenses	
5600 – Purchases	

Start date	✓
20/01/20X3	
28/01/20X3	
28/02/20X3	
28/12/20X3	

Frequency	✓
Weekly	
Monthly	
Quarterly	
Annually	

End date	✓
20/01/20X4	
28/01/20X4	
28/02/20X4	
28/12/20X3	

(5 marks)

(b)   Which ONE of the following is true regarding recurring entries in a computerised bookkeeping system?

	✓
The system makes sure the entries will be in the correct codes	
There is no scope for human error	
Entries will be made that automatically balance	
Individuals will still have to manually balance the cash book	

(1 mark)

TASK 10 (10 MARKS)

This task is about transferring data from the books of prime entry.

Today's date is 31 January 20X3 and you are responsible for transferring entries from the daybooks to the general ledger.

The totals of the purchases daybook of Pontoon Co are shown below. Some of the entries for transferring the item to the general ledger below have been filled in.

Date 20X3	Details	Total £	VAT £	Net £
31 Jan	Totals	6,804.00	1,134.00	5,670.00

(a)   **What will be the entries in the general ledger?**

Account name	Amount £	Debit ✓	Credit ✓
Purchases			
VAT	1,134		
Payables ledger control			

(5 marks)

The totals of the discounts received daybook of Pontoon Co are shown below. Some of the entries for transferring the item to the general ledger below have been filled in.

Date 20X3	Details	Total £	VAT £	Net £
31 Jan	Totals	408	68	340

(b)   **What will be the entries in the general ledger?**

Account name	Amount £	Debit ✓	Credit ✓
Discounts received			
VAT	68		
Payables ledger control			

(5 marks)

TASK 11 (10 MARKS)

This task is about totalling and balancing ledger accounts.

The customer account below is ready to be totalled and balanced at 31 January 20X3.

Swain Ltd

Date 20X3	Details	Amount £	Date 20X3	Details	Amount £
3 Jan	Invoice 932	9,450	8 Jan	Payment	14,630
9 Jan	Invoice 984	6,430			
16 Jan	Invoice 993	4,240			

(a)   Identify the entry required to record the closing balance on 31 January 20X3.

Detail	Amount £	Debit ✓	Credit ✓

Detail picklist: Balance b/d, balance c/d

(3 marks)

(b)   Calculate the amount that will be entered in each debit and credit column after the closing balance has been recorded.

£

(1 mark)

(c)   On which side of the ledger account would each item be shown in a supplier's ledger account?

Details	Debit ✓	Credit ✓
Purchase		
Discount received		
Payment made		

(3 marks)

(d)   On which side would the opening balance be recorded for each of the following accounts?

Details	Debit ✓	Credit ✓
Land & buildings		
Capital		
Loan from bank		

(3 marks)

Section 4

MOCK ASSESSMENT ANSWERS

TASK 1 (10 MARKS)

This task is about manual and digital bookkeeping systems.

(a) **Which document or report would be used for each of the purposes below?**

	Document or report
To identify which specific invoices are being paid off when sending payment	Remittance
To issue a refund, write off an amount owed following a return of goods	Credit note
To show the detail of the goods sold and total price	Sales invoice
To show details of the amounts owed from each customer	Receivables ledger

(4 marks)

(b) **Identify the correct product codes for the items below.**

Product	Product Code
Aeroplane	01AE
Astronaut	03AS
Alphabet Blocks	02AL

(2 marks)

Feedback: The correct alphabetical order here is Aeroplane, Alphabet blocks, Astronaut

(c) **Identify whether the following statements regarding manual bookkeeping systems are true or false.**

	True	False
The sales returns daybook is one of the books of prime entry	✓	
A manual bookkeeping system can decrease the risk of errors when moving data from the books of prime entry to the ledgers		✓

(2 marks)

Feedback: Human error is possible when transferring data from daybooks to the ledgers in a manual system

(d)   Identify whether the following statements regarding digital bookkeeping systems are true or false

	True	False
A digital bookkeeping system automatically reconciles receivables and payables ledgers to the control accounts	✓	
A digital bookkeeping system automatically balances the cash book	✓	

(2 marks)

TASK 2 (10 MARKS)

This task is about principles of double-entry bookkeeping.

(a)   Identify the classification of each account.

Account	Classification
Trade payable	Liability
Computer equipment	Asset
Discounts received	Income

(3 marks)

(b)   Calculate the amount of assets in Pontoon Co.

£51,040

(1 mark)

Feedback:

Assets – Liabilities = Capital

Therefore, Assets = Capital + liabilities = £16,540 + £34.500 = £51,040

(c)   Identify the dual effect of each transaction by matching the dual effect from the picklist to the transaction identified. You should ignore VAT in this task.

Transaction	Dual effect
A sale of goods on credit	Increase in assets and income
Received a new loan from the bank	Increase in assets and liabilities
Payment to a credit supplier using the bank	Decrease in assets and liabilities
A purchase of a motor vehicle for cash	Both increase and decrease an asset
Payment of fuel expenses for cash	Increase in expenses, decrease in assets
Receipt of cash from the owner	Increase in assets and capital

(6 marks)

Feedback:

A sale of goods on credit: Dr Receivables, Cr Revenue. Received a new loan: Dr Cash, Cr Loan liability. Payment to a credit supplier: Dr Payables, Cr Cash. Purchase MV: Dr Non-current assets, Cr Cash. Payment for fuel: Dr Fuel expense, Cr Cash. Receipt of cash from the owner: Dr Cash, Cr Capital

TASK 3 (10 MARKS)

This task is about processing customer invoices or credit notes and entering in daybooks.

(a)   **Calculate the amounts to be included in the invoice.**

	£
Amount before discount	20,000
Discount given	(2,000)
Amount after discount	18,000
VAT	3,600
Total	21,600

(5 marks)

(b)   **Which daybook will the above transaction be entered in?**

	✓
Sales daybook	✓
Sales returns daybook	
Cash book	
Discounts allowed daybook	

(1 mark)

(c)   **Complete the daybook entry below**

Date 20X2	Customer code	Invoice No:	Total £	VAT £	Net £
1 Dec	JJ01	142	21,600	3,600	18,000

(4 marks)

TASK 4 (10 MARKS)

This task is about processing receipts from customers.

(a)   **Complete the following statement:**

Buckley Co has _____GAP 1_____ so _____GAP 2_____.

Gap 1	✓
Overpaid Pontoon Co	✓
Underpaid Pontoon Co	
Paid Pontoon Co the correct amount	

Gap 2	✓
A refund is due	✓
A request for further payment should be made	
No further action is required	

(2 marks)

Feedback: Buckley Co should have paid Pontoon Co £173 (£144 + £54 – £25)

(b) **Complete the following statement:**

Moran Co has _____GAP 1_____ so _____GAP 2_____.

Gap 1	✓
Overpaid Pontoon Co	
Underpaid Pontoon Co	✓
Paid Pontoon Co the correct amount	

Gap 2	✓
A refund is due	
A request for further payment should be made	✓
No further action is required	

(2 marks)

Feedback: Moran Co should have paid Pontoon Co £504 (£288 + £216). As the invoices were paid after 20 days, no prompt payment discount is applicable

(c) **If Moran Co pays the above invoice within 10 days and receives the prompt payment discount, what is the amount that Moran Co will pay?**

£688.75

(1 mark)

Feedback: (£725× 95%) = £688.75

(d) **How would Pontoon Co categorise the discount taken by Moran Co?**

	✓
Income	
Expense	✓
Asset	
Liability	

(1 mark)

(e) **Which TWO errors have Pontoon Co made in the above invoice?**

	✓
The total product cost is incorrectly calculated	
The bulk discount should not be applied until Pontoon Co know if the payment will be made on time	
The VAT figure is incorrectly calculated	✓
The total invoice amount is incorrectly calculated	✓

(2 marks)

Feedback:

The VAT should be on the net amount = £162 × 20% = £32.40

The VAT has been subtracted in error, rather than added to the invoice total

(f) **Identify if the invoices have been paid correctly or not**

	Paid correctly	Not paid correctly
Invoice 145	✓	
Invoice 183		✓

(2 marks)

Feedback: The VAT on Invoice 183 has not been paid

TASK 5 (10 MARKS)

(a) **Enter the details into the missing sections in the daybook**

Date 20X2	Supplier code	Invoice No:	Total £	VAT £	Net £
10 Dec	CLA05	1365	3,312.00	552.00	2,760.00

(4 marks)

(b) **Which daybook would this be entered into?**

	✓
Suppliers daybook	
Purchases daybook	✓
Cash book	
Sales daybook	

(1 mark)

(c) **Which TWO of these items represent the dual effect in Pontoon Co's records when the credit note is received?**

	✓
Liabilities will decrease	✓
Assets will increase	
Expenses will decrease	✓
Income will increase	

(2 marks)

Feedback: Dr Payables, Cr Purchase expense

(d)   Identify the THREE discrepancies between the purchase order and the purchase invoice

	✓
Net amount	
VAT calculation	✓
Total amount	✓
Payment terms	✓
Product supplied	
Quantity supplied	
Unit price	

(3 marks)

Feedback: The PO has no VAT calculation and no total amount given. The invoice payment date is less than the 30 days on the purchase order

TASK 6 (10 MARKS)

This task is about processing payments to suppliers.

(a)   Calculate the amount to be paid to each supplier if the prompt payment discount is taken and when the payment needs to be made.

Supplier	£	Date by which to make the payment
Groves Ltd	1,368.00	13 January
Moore Ltd	982.80	8 January

(4 marks)

Feedback:

Groves Ltd £1,440 × 95% = £1368.00. Moore Ltd £1,092 × 90% = £982.80

(b)   Which FOUR items should now be removed from the Bloomer Ltd customer statement now that the payment has been made?

Details	✓
Invoice 345	✓
Invoice 346	✓
Invoice 347	✓
Credit note 101	✓
Invoice 348	
Invoice 349	
Credit note 102	

(4 marks)

Feedback: £10,450 + £3,210 + £2,000 − £1,030 = £14,630

(c) **What will be the amount remaining as owed to Bloomer Ltd?**

£1,000

(1 mark)

Feedback: £230 + £820 − £50 = £1,000

(d) **Which of the following statements regarding remittance advices is correct?**

Details	✓
Remittance advices will be sent to the inventory department to advise them inventory has been paid for	
Remittance advices will be sent to the customer to advise them of the amount being paid	
Remittance advices will be sent to the bank to confirm payment is to be made	
Remittance advices will be sent to the supplier to advise them of the amount being paid	✓

(1 mark)

TASK 7 (8 MARKS)

Update the extract from the receipts section of the cash book below.

Details	General ledger code	Total £	VAT £	Net £
Broomes Co	3463 Trade Receivables	7,200	1,200	6,000
Cash sales	6200 Sales	560	0	560

(8 marks)

TASK 8 (6 MARKS)

(a) **What will be the entries required at 31 January to restore the total of the petty cash back up to £300?**

Details	Amount £	Debit ✓	Credit ✓
Cash from bank	75.00	✓	

(3 marks)

Feedback: £60 + £15 = £75 paid into petty cash

(b) **What is the entry made in the petty cash book to record the closing balance on 30th June?**

Details	Amount £	Debit ✓	Credit ✓
Balance c/d	300.00		✓

(3 marks)

Feedback: £300 will be in petty cash. As an asset it will be b/d on the debit side on 1 July and hence is c/d on the credit side at 30 June

TASK 9 (6 MARKS)

(a) **Set up the recurring entry**

Transaction type	Details	Start date	Frequency	End date	Amount £
Recurring payment	1560 – Office expenses	28/01/20X3	Monthly	28/12/20X3	55.00

(5 marks)

Feedback: The monthly payment is £660/12 = £55

(b) **Which ONE of the following is true regarding recurring entries in a computerised bookkeeping system?**

	✓
The system makes sure the entries will be in the correct codes	
There is no scope for human error	
Entries will be made that automatically balance	✓
Individuals will still have to manually balance the cash book	

(1 mark)

TASK 10 (10 MARKS)

(a) **What will be the entries in the general ledger?**

Account name	Amount £	Debit ✓	Credit ✓
Purchases	5,670	✓	
VAT	1,134	✓	
Payables ledger control	6,804		✓

(5 marks)

(b) **What will be the entries in the general ledger?**

Account name	Amount £	Debit ✓	Credit ✓
Discounts received	340		✓
VAT	68		✓
Payables ledger control	408	✓	

(5 marks)

Feedback: A discount received reduces the amount of input VAT we can reclaim from HMRC and hence is a credit to the VAT control account

TASK 11 (10 MARKS)

(a) **Identify the entry required to record the closing balance on 31 January 20X3.**

Detail	Amount £	Debit ✓	Credit ✓
Balance c/d	5,490		✓

(3 marks)

Feedback:

Swain Ltd

Date 20X3	Details	Amount £	Date 20X3	Details	Amount £
3 Jan	Invoice 932	9,450	8 Jan	Payment	14,630
9 Jan	Invoice 984	6,430			
16 Jan	Invoice 993	4,240		Balance c/d	5,490
		20,120			20,120
	Balance b/d	5,490			

(b) **Calculate the amount that will be entered in each debit and credit column after the closing balance has been recorded.**

£20,120

(1 mark)

(c)   On which side of the ledger account would each item be shown in a supplier's ledger account?

Details	Debit ✓	Credit ✓
Credit purchase		✓
Discount received	✓	
Payment made	✓	

(3 marks)

(d)   On which side would the opening balance be recorded for each of the following accounts?

Details	Debit ✓	Credit ✓
Land & buildings	✓	
Capital		✓
Loan from bank		✓

(3 marks)